*International Political Economy Series*

General Editor: Timothy M. Shaw, Professor and Director, Institute of International Relations, The University of the West Indies, Trinidad & Tobago

*Titles include:*

Hans Abrahamsson
UNDERSTANDING WORLD ORDER AND STRUCTURAL CHANGE
Poverty, Conflict and the Global Arena

Morten Bøås, Marianne H. Marchand and Timothy Shaw *(editors)*
THE POLITICAL ECONOMY OF REGIONS AND REGIONALISM

James Busumtwi-Sam and Laurent Dobuzinskis
TURBULENCE AND NEW DIRECTION IN GLOBAL POLITICAL ECONOMY

Bill Dunn
GLOBAL RESTRUCTURING AND THE POWER OF LABOUR

Myron J. Frankman
WORLD DEMOCRATIC FEDERALISM
Peace and Justice Indivisible

Barry K. Gills *(editor)*
GLOBALIZATION AND THE POLITICS OF RESISTANCE

Richard Grant and John Rennie Short *(editors)*
GLOBALIZATION AND THE MARGINS

Graham Harrison *(editor)*
GLOBAL ENCOUNTERS
International Political Economy, Development and Globalization

Patrick Hayden and Chamsy el-Ojeili *(editors)*
CONFRONTING GLOBALIZATION
Humanity, Justice and the Renewal of Politics

Axel Hülsemeyer *(editor)*
GLOBALIZATION IN THE TWENTY–FIRST CENTURY
Convergence or Divergence?

Helge Hveem and Kristen Nordhaug *(editors)*
PUBLIC POLICY IN THE AGE OF GLOBALIZATION
Responses to Environmental and Economic Crises

Jomo K.S. and Shyamala Nagaraj *(editors)*
GLOBALIZATION VERSUS DEVELOPMENT

Adrian Kay and Owain David Williams *(editors)*
GLOBAL HEALTH GOVERNANCE
Crisis, Institutions and Political Economy

Dominic Kelly and Wyn Grant *(editors)*
THE POLITICS OF INTERNATIONAL TRADE IN THE 21ST CENTURY
Actors, Issues and Regional Dynamics

Sandra J. MacLean, Sherri A. Brown and Pieter Fourie *(editors)*
HEALTH FOR SOME
The Political Economy of Global Health Governance

Craig N. Murphy *(editor)*
EGALITARIAN POLITICS IN THE AGE OF GLOBALIZATION

John Nauright and Kimberly S. Schimmel *(editors)*
THE POLITICAL ECONOMY OF SPORT

Morten Ougaard
THE GLOBALIZATION OF POLITICS
Power, Social Forces and Governance

Jørgen Dige Pedersen
GLOBALIZATION, DEVELOPMENT AND THE STATE
The Performance of India and Brazil Since 1990

Markus Perkmann and Ngai-Ling Sum
GLOBALIZATION, REGIONALIZATION AND CROSS-BORDER REGIONS

K Ravi Raman and Ronnie D. Lipschutz (*editors*)
CORPORATE SOCIAL RESPONSIBILITY
Comparative Critiques

Ben Richardson
SUGAR: REFINED POWER IN A GLOBAL REGIME

Marc Schelhase
GLOBALIZATION, REGIONALIZATION AND BUSINESS
Conflict, Convergence and Influence

Herman M. Schwartz and Leonard Seabrooke (*editors*)
THE POLITICS OF HOUSING BOOMS AND BUSTS

Leonard Seabrooke
US POWER IN INTERNATIONAL FINANCE
The Victory of Dividends

Timothy J. Sinclair and Kenneth P. Thomas (*editors*)
STRUCTURE AND AGENCY IN INTERNATIONAL CAPITAL MOBILITY

J.P. Singh (*editor*)
INTERNATIONAL CULTURAL POLICIES AND POWER

Fredrik Söderbaum and Timothy M. Shaw (*editors*)
THEORIES OF NEW REGIONALISM

Susanne Soederberg, Georg Menz and Philip G. Cerny (*editors*)
INTERNALIZING GLOBALIZATION
The Rise of Neoliberalism and the Decline of National Varieties of Capitalism

Helen Thompson
CHINA AND THE MORTGAGING OF AMERICA
Economic Interdependence and Domestic Politics

Ritu Vij (*editor*)
GLOBALIZATION AND WELFARE
A Critical Reader

Matthew Watson
THE POLITICAL ECONOMY OF INTERNATIONAL CAPITAL MOBILITY

Owen Worth and Phoebe Moore
GLOBALIZATION AND THE 'NEW' SEMI-PERIPHERIES

---

**International Political Economy Series**
**Series Standing Order ISBN 978–0–333–71708–0 hardcover**
**Series Standing Order ISBN 978–0–333–71110–1 paperback**

You can receive future titles in this series as they are published by placing a standing order. Please contact your bookseller or, in case of difficulty, write to us at the address below with your name and address, the title of the series and one of the ISBNs quoted above.

Customer Services Department, Macmillan Distribution Ltd, Houndmills, Basingstoke, Hampshire RG21 6XS, England

---

# China and the Mortgaging of America

## Economic Interdependence and Domestic Politics

Helen Thompson
*University of Cambridge, UK*

palgrave
macmillan

First published 2010 by
PALGRAVE MACMILLAN

Palgrave Macmillan in the UK is an imprint of Macmillan Publishers Limited, registered in England, company number 785998, of Houndmills, Basingstoke, Hampshire RG21 6XS.

Palgrave Macmillan in the US is a division of St Martin's Press LLC, 175 Fifth Avenue, New York, NY 10010.

Palgrave Macmillan is the global academic imprint of the above companies and has companies and representatives throughout the world.

Palgrave® and Macmillan® are registered trademarks in the United States, the United Kingdom, Europe and other countries

ISBN 978-0-230-24359-0 hardback

This book is printed on paper suitable for recycling and made from fully managed and sustained forest sources. Logging, pulping and manufacturing processes are expected to conform to the environmental regulations of the country of origin.

A catalogue record for this book is available from the British Library.

A catalogue record for this book is available from the Library of Congress.

10 9 8 7 6 5 4 3 2 1
19 18 17 16 15 14 13 12 11 10

Printed and bound in Great Britain by
CPI Antony Rowe, Chippenham and Eastbourne

*For Geoffrey Hawthorn*

# Contents

# List of Tables

# Preface

I began this book in the last months of 2008, as the financial crisis appeared to risk pushing the world economy into a crisis not seen since the inter-war years. I started from the sense that there was something not quite right in much that I was reading about the crisis and its causes, and that the political atmosphere of those months was obscuring some important truths about what had happened. Some of that distortion came from a failure to see or comprehend what the place of the two state-supported American mortgage corporations, Fannie Mae and Freddie Mac, had been in what had transpired over the previous 18 months. It was in what happened to these hugely indebted two corporations that the mortgage boom, the wider financial bubble, and the international flows of capital from China to the United States had come together most sharply and consequentially. And it was in a crisis in September 2008 generated for the American government by the inability of these two corporations to meet their debt obligations to the east Asian central banks that the whole effective structure of the international economy over the past decade had stood in most jeopardy from the financial crisis that had been brewing since the previous summer. This book is an attempt to explain how that crisis came about, what its implications were, and what these things say about the nature of economic interdependence today.

I have incurred several of my own debts in writing this book. My thanks go to Steven Kennedy, Alexandra Webster, and Renée Takken at Palgrave for their efficiency and encouragement, and Timothy Shaw, the editor of the International Political Economy series, for his enthusiasm for the project. Two anonymous reviewers gave some very helpful suggestions. Brad Setser kindly helped me with the data on Russia's official dollar holdings. Bear McCreary's extraordinary music was a constant companion. David Runciman and Geoffrey Hawthorn encouraged me to write this book when in various ways I was all too readily going in less productive directions. Geoffrey Hawthorn also quite rightly forced me to get to grips with some problems in the last chapter. As always, I am deeply grateful to them both.

Helen Thompson

# Abbreviations

| | |
|---|---|
| AIG | American International Group |
| APEC | Asia-Pacific Economic Co-operation |
| APT | ASEAN plus Three |
| ASEAN | Association of South East Asian Nations |
| CIC | China Investment Corporation |
| CMI | Chiang Mai Initiative |
| CRA | Community Reinvestment Act |
| EU | European Union |
| FDI | Foreign Direct Investment |
| FHA | Federal Housing Administration |
| FHFA | Federal Housing Finance Agency |
| GATT | General Agreement on Tariffs and Trade |
| GDP | Gross Domestic Product |
| GSE | Government Sponsored Enterprise |
| HOLC | Home Owners' Loan Corporation |
| IMF | International Monetary Fund |
| NINA | No Income, No Assets |
| OECD | Organization for Economic Cooperation and Development |
| OFHEO | Office of Federal Housing Enterprise Oversight |
| RFC | Reconstruction Finance Corporation |
| TARP | Troubled Assets Relief Programme |
| WTO | World Trade Organisation |

# 1
# Introduction

In late August 2008, two congressionally-chartered American mortgage corporations, Fannie Mae and Freddie Mac, were facing imminent debt repayments that they could not meet. Between them they owned or guaranteed around 50 per cent of all American mortgages and they had $5.4 trillion of liabilities in securities and bonds. Their primary creditors included the Chinese and Japanese central banks. These two central banks had purchased the two corporations' debt and securities because they believed that in the final instance the American government would take responsibility for these liabilities. But, in the summer of 2008, the Chinese and Japanese central banks, and many of Fannie Mae and Freddie Mac's other creditors, were not willing to expose that faith any further and were selling a significant amount of their holdings of the corporations' bonds and securities. With the two corporations unable to raise new capital, the American mortgage market, which since the middle of 2007 had come to rest largely on them, was frozen. And with foreign creditors selling significant quantities of one set of dollar assets, the prevailing international economy that had sustained ever-rising western living standards and taken millions of people in developing countries out of poverty over the past two decades stood on the precipice of collapse.

The crisis around Fannie Mae and Freddie Mac in the summer of 2008 was the first serious test of the economic relationship that had developed between the United States and east Asia since the turn of the century. Either the American government acted to guarantee the corporations' debt, or the Japanese and Chinese central banks would have unwound large swathes of their overall dollar holdings and plunged the whole international economy into an immense crisis. On 7 September 2008, the Bush administration accepted what the Chinese and Japanese governments had hoped was always the inevitable outcome of this crisis and put the two corporations into conservatorship whilst guaranteeing full payments to bond and security holders. In saving Fannie Mae and Freddie Mac, the Bush administration took onto the Treasury's liabilities a sum equal to the entire federal debt of the United States and assumed *de facto* direct responsibility for trying to resurrect new lending in the American mortgage market. Yet the conservatorship was not sufficient to restore the confidence of the Asian central banks, and after the Treasury's September announcement, they continued to sell. With private investors and foreign central banks unwilling to offer any new credit, the Federal Reserve Board was left to promise to buy more of the bonds issued and securities guaranteed by Fannie Mae and Freddie Mac. In practice, this meant that the American central bank was printing money to rescue a mortgage market that could no longer be sustained by foreign credit.

Ten years previously such a crisis could not have happened because the financial aspects of the economic relationship between the United States and east Asia were almost entirely otherwise. Indeed in the summer of 1998 the prevailing economic relationship between east Asia and the United States had been defined by a thoroughly different kind of crisis, one shaped by a huge exit of foreign capital out of east Asia and the terms that the United States had demanded, via the International Monetary Fund (IMF), for bailing out several of the east Asian states. Then the problems of corporations servicing debt owed abroad and the domestic and international economic and political problems that generated belonged to east Asia not the United States. The 2008 crisis, however, was far from a straight reversal of the one of 1997–98. Many east Asian corporations had borrowed in a foreign currency and their debt problems had begun with a currency crisis. Since the turn of the century, by contrast, the United States had become the debtor and the east Asian states creditors in the financial relationship between them without the east Asian states assuming the political strength that accrues to states that can lend in their own currency. In becoming large-scale creditors the east Asian states created new economic and political problems for themselves, just as the United States confronted problems it had not encountered in its previous experiences as a debtor.

The events of summer 2008, and the escalation of the financial crisis that followed, significantly changed, once again, the economic relationship between the United States and the east Asian states, and China in particular. Although the American government acted to avoid the meltdown that would have ensued if it had refused to guarantee Fannie Mae and Freddie Mac's debts, it could not re-establish the old *status quo* in the relationship that had made it possible for the Asian central banks to finance much of the American mortgage boom. Whilst the short-term economic interests of the east Asian states continued to bind them to the financial relationship, the Chinese government, in particular, now had considerable reasons to fear the consequences of maintaining that relationship. For its part, the American state was left, by the end, of 2008, carrying the burden of a huge amount of peacetime debt. The scale of that debt and the fiscal problems it would generate could only give the Chinese government even more reason to fear what lay economically ahead. The crisis also reshaped the domestic political space in which each government had to manage the economic relationship with the other, and in doing so, made the relationship even more fraught and vulnerable to future crisis.

## The economic relationship between the United States and East Asia from the 1990s to the summer of 2008: An overview

The broad contours of the international economy during the 1990s were shaped by the conjunction of deepening trade and capital flows, and the post-cold war reach of American power. For different states the consequences of this particular kind of international economy in this particular geo-political setting played out differently. For the east Asian states, they proved both very advantageous and a burden. The expansion of international trade, the proliferation of regional trade agreements, and the surge in foreign direct investment during the 1990s, created strong incentives for governments to pursue particular kinds of economic policies. In this sense the international economy was a severe constraint on states. Governments that wished to regulate labour markets, or levy comparatively high rates of corporate taxation, or finance welfare and health programmes with significant employer contributions risked making their economies unattractive to long-term investors. However, the expansion of international trade and capital flows were also an opportunity, and one that many of the east Asian states grabbed more successfully than any other states. They expanded trade with each other, drew large quantities of foreign direct investment, and exported manufactured goods into western markets, in particular to the United States. Although, after its spectacular success in earlier decades, the Japanese economy slumped through the 1990s, most east Asian states enjoyed high levels of growth through the first two-thirds of the decade.

However, even for the most economically successful, like the east Asian, the vast movements of short-term capital flows that had come to characterise the post-Bretton Woods international economy and the primacy of the dollar as a *de facto* international currency created a structural problem around exchange rates, which both imposed a serious constraint on macro-economic policy options and risked wrecking export-led growth strategies. Whilst governments could decide to make decisions about monetary and fiscal policy independently of the position of their currency, to do so risked deleterious economic outcomes either in terms of inflation or growth and employment. Different states had tried different approaches to try to establish some autonomy from the day-to-day volatility of fast-moving foreign exchange markets. The European Union (EU) states had run in the European Exchange Rate Mechanism a collective pegged exchange rate system that allowed each individual currency to float against the dollar. Others, like Argentina, had adopted a currency board, which effectively stripped the state of any monetary autonomy. Japan aside, the east Asian states had run various forms of pegs against the dollar and directed their monetary policy to try to maintain at least some measure of exchange rate stability. For its part, the Japanese government had struggled to find any solution to the problem since the second half of the 1980s. The experience of the Japanese government showed just what an economic liability the exchange rate problem could be when it could not be managed to achieve an end a government and central bank had set for themselves. With persistent upward market pressure on the yen, the export competitiveness of the Japanese economy deteriorated and under

American political pressure to loosen monetary policy, the Japanese government was left fuelling a domestic bubble that needed to be checked. In the wake of the Japanese government's inability to solve these exchange rate generated problems, the Japanese economy spent most of the 1990s mired between modest growth and recession and eventually fell into a period, extending into the next decade, of sustained deflation.[1]

The capacity of the United States to exercise power in the international economy of the 1990s, especially in the monetary and financial sphere, was significantly greater than it had been over the previous few decades. The post-Bretton Woods international economy had long given the United States considerable structural financial power. It held the pre-eminent international currency, it was free to pursue whatever dollar policy it wished without the constraint of any multilateral agreements of the kind that had constricted American macroeconomic policy during the 1950s and 1960s, and it could use the IMF to determine the terms of credit to states suffering from balance of payments problems. During the 1990s the demise of the Soviet Union and the superiority of the United States' economic performance over Japan and Germany gave American Presidents the opportunity to demand more from other states for the economic benefits that the United States provided in the form of access to its domestic market and to capital of one kind or another. They used that power to open other states' financial markets, to attach more stringent conditionality attached to credit whether in bilateral arrangements, like with Mexico in 1995, or via the IMF, as with Russia in 1998–1999. In the case of Mexico, the terms of the loan, not least the rate of interest which Washington charged, were so tough that the Mexican government used only a tiny part of the loan granted and repaid at the first opportunity.[2]

Perhaps nowhere in the world was the revamped reach of America power more apparent than in east Asia.[3] In 1993, the Clinton administration imposed a trade agreement on the Japanese government that required it to make structural reforms to several sectors of the Japanese economy. A year later, the Clinton administration pushed the members of the Asian Pacific Economic Co-operation (APEC) into a commitment to create a free trade and investment area. In 1996 it insisted to the South Korean government that a timetable for financial liberalisation was a necessary condition of membership of the OECD. During the Asian financial crisis, Clinton administration officials were involved in an unprecedented manner in the negotiations between the IMF and the three states that turned to the Fund for large loans. In the case of South Korea, Washington pushed the IMF to demand more foreign ownership, external access to domestic banks, reforms to the central bank, western practices of accounting, a restructuring of the country's largest companies, new labour laws, and a tacit promise that nobody should run for the impending presidential elections who did not support the IMF loan.[4] Although, Indonesia aside, the east Asian states recovered relatively quickly from the Asian financial crisis, the economies of those that did so on the back of IMF support had, in doing so, become significantly more open to American capital and goods and with it more constrained by the various problems wrought by economic interdependence. In the aftermath of the crisis, the Clinton administration then procured the acquiescence of the Chinese government to an extraordinarily tough set of conditions for membership of the World Trade Organisation (WTO).[5]

By contrast, during the first few years of the 21st century, there was a set of developments that in their cumulative impact diminished the United States' capacity to exercise power in the international economy. In part the problems that American monetary and financial dominance of the international economy had produced for other states during the 1980s and 1990s pushed other states to try to increase their autonomy in relation to the United States. For much of the EU, the formation of the euro reduced the problems of exchange rate management caused by the dollar for the operation of the Exchange Rate Mechanism. More importantly for others, it created a possible long-term alternative to the dollar as the world's premier reserve currency.[6] Although there was little reason to suppose that the euro constituted any immediate threat to the dollar, it increased the options open to other states in accumulating portfolios of foreign exchange reserves.[7] Meanwhile various states turned away from the IMF to escape American strictures on their domestic decision-making. Many of those states that took large loans from the IMF between 1990 and 2001 repaid them early, such that the amount of loans outstanding to the IMF fell dramatically between the end of 2002 and the end of 2006. With the exception of Turkey, none of the larger emerging-market states has taken a new loan from the IMF since Brazil did in 2002.[8]

However, in part the changes in the power dynamics of the international economy since the Asian financial crisis were also driven by the spectacular growth of the Chinese economy, particularly between 2003 and 2008. That economic success was primarily based on trade, with China enjoying a rate of growth in exports frequently double its overall annual rate of growth. The consequences for other states of China's economic rise were profound in a range of spheres. China's demand for energy helped to produce a large increase in the price of oil after 2002, which put pressure on the balance of payments of energy-importing states and gave energy-rich states a financial windfall and the opportunity to assert themselves externally against the United States. Cheap Chinese imports mitigated against the inflationary pressures created by the rise in the price of oil, but they also threatened domestic producers in other states that could not compete on cost. The speed at which Chinese exports grew created new protectionist demands in the EU and, in particular, the United States. Meanwhile, the Chinese government proved an alternative source of credit for developing-country states, especially in Africa. Whilst the international financial institutions and the United States had in the post-cold war era made borrowing dependent on human rights performance, the Chinese government was willing to eschew political conditionality in its search for secure energy and mineral supplies.[9]

These developments impacted to varying degrees on east Asia. In some ways, they tightened the constraints of economic interdependence. Monetarily and trade-wise, the east Asian economies were bound to the dollar and had to absorb the fallout of whatever relationship between the dollar and the euro in the foreign exchange markets ensued. For its parts, China's rise created a new set of interdependencies between China and the other east Asian economies. By the middle of the decade, China had become the hub of the Asian regional economy. The Japanese and Chinese economies had become particularly dependent on each other, with China providing Japan with new exports markets, which proved crucial to Japan's post-2004 economic recovery, and Japan acting as the largest single foreign investor in China. Politically, the east Asian states were themselves part of the reaction against the way the United States had exercised its monetary and financial power during the 1990s. Thailand and South Korea repaid the loans they had taken during the financial crisis early and Indonesia declined further credit when its 2000–3 deal expired. During the Asian financial crisis, the three large north-east Asian states – China, Japan and South Korea – had agreed to form an organisation with the members of ASEAN known as ASEAN plus Three (APT). In 2000, the ATP states moved to create a fledging currency swap system. This was nowhere the radical move that the Japanese government had wished to make during the financial crisis itself, when it had proposed establishing an autonomous Asian Monetary Fund. Nonetheless, it did demonstrate that the east Asian states had found a new will to collective co-operation, which crucially included China, in the face of the financial and exchange rate risks inherent both to the prevailing terms of economic interdependence and the capacity of the United States to use its power against other states' economic interests.

In this changing international economy, a particular relationship emerged between the United States and east Asia in which the American consumer market underpinned the east Asian states, especially China's pursuit of export-led growth and east Asia acted as a large-scale creditor to the United States. The trade part of this relationship followed an existing historical pattern, which dated back to first Japan and then South Korea's post-war development and which had operated in much the same way for the later industrialising states during the late 1980s and 1990s. The east Asian states used access to the American market as part of a drive for export-led rapid growth. In China's case, in sharp contrast to the policies pursued by the Japanese government during the post-war period, this trade strategy was complemented by an openness to American direct investment, much of which went into the export-oriented sectors of the economy.

The financial and monetary relationship that emerged between the United States and the east Asian states in the early years of the 21st century was born out of the conjunction of the Asian experience of the Asian financial crisis, the Chinese government's development strategy, and the borrowing requirements of the United States. The fallout of the capital flight out of east Asia in the second half of 1997 and 1998 was traumatic. It had wrought severe recession across the region, wrecked most of the dollar pegs that in different ways the east Asian states had tried to maintain since the beginning of the 1990s, and produced the political humiliation of the IMF experience. Although capital controls had ensured that the Chinese economy had suffered far less than others, the Chinese government drew much the same conclusions as their east Asian counterparts about what avoiding a repetition of the crisis required. First and foremost, the east Asian governments decided to protect their currencies from future speculative attack by accumulating large-scale foreign exchange reserves and none did so more determinedly than China. In practice this meant that from 2002 the east Asian central banks, and the Chinese and Japanese in particular, bought an enormous amount of American Treasury bonds and the bonds and securities issued by Fannie Mae and Freddie Mac. In the year prior to the Asian financial crisis, China was estimated to have held around $100 billion worth of foreign exchange reserves. By the end of 2008, that figure was in excess of $2 trillion, a more than 20-fold increase. Second, the east Asian states moved to create current account surpluses in the belief that states with current account deficits were more prone to currency speculation. Third, they sought to establish what Ronald McKinnon has described as an East Asian dollar standard. For most states this meant, in his words, 'informal dollar pegging'.[10] This remained most difficult for Japan. For China, which had been able to maintain its formal peg during the financial crisis, it meant retaining that peg whilst accumulating what would become a large current account surplus. This east Asian dollar standard backed by large-scale foreign exchange reserves had a direct trade benefit because it allowed the east Asian states both to keep their currencies at levels against the dollar that enhanced their export competitiveness in dollar-denominated external markets even as they earned sizeable current account surpluses and to maintain regional exchange rate stability to encourage rapidly expanding intra-east Asian trade, most of which was denominated in dollars.[11]

However strong the east Asian desire to save so much of their export earnings and invest them in short-term dollar assets, the opportunity to execute this foreign economic strategy depended on a parallel need for capital in the United States. This American demand for capital arose on two fronts. The United States has been continuously dependent on foreign capital in one form or another since the early 1980s when it had begun running a persistent current account deficit. At times that need for capital has been accentuated by the decision of Presidents and Congress to run significant budget deficits in the absence of significant domestic savings. From the mid-1990s, the American current account deficit steadily deteriorated, rising to more than 6 per cent of Gross Domestic Product (GDP) in 2006. Meanwhile, the American federal budget moved from a surplus in 1998–2000 to a deficit of nearly 5 per cent in 2003.

The financial side of the economic relationship with east Asia was a boon to the United States. After 2000, the United States was able to procure a vast amount of cheap capital. Whilst the United States has enjoyed privileges as a debtor since its ascendancy to monetary power after the First World War, the terms on which it could finance these twin deficits from east Asia were exceptional. In 2003, the Federal Reserve Board was able to hold interest rates at between 1 and 1.25 per cent, a level not seen since the immediate years after the Second World War. By contrast, the financial and monetary side of the relationship with the United States left the east Asian states with some severe problems. They had turned themselves into being large-scale creditor states that could not lend in their own currencies to recycle their export earnings. This is what McKinnon has called 'the syndrome of conflicted virtue'.[12] Since the widening size of the American current account deficit suggested that the dollar would depreciate over time and their lending facilitated very low American interest rates, in lending in dollars the east Asian states were both securing a very small return on their savings and incurring a significant risk that the local currency value of their assets would depreciate over time. Meanwhile, since they earned large current account surpluses, they invited pressure from deficit states, not least the United States itself. In terms of financial incentives alone the east Asian states were doing something that was perverse, and in terms of the trade benefits that made the financial relationship rational they were doing something that risked its own destruction.

For these reasons, some scholars and commentators saw the economic relationship that had emerged by the middle of the decade as fraught, whatever the short-term trade benefits to east Asia or the need for capital of the United States. Lawrence Summers memorably described it as 'a balance of financial terror'[13] because each side had the capacity to inflict huge damage on the other. The Asian states could stop lending or sell their dollar assets should they fear that the dollar was weakening beyond their ability to reverse that weakness. The United States could allow the dollar to depreciate substantially over time to repay its foreign debt and improve its balance of payments, or default on some part of its debt, and erect new tariffs against Asian exports to stem domestic anger about Asia's trade surpluses. That either side had not hitherto acted in any of these ways was because each understood the depth of their exposure to the other. Others countered that the crucial fact about this economic relationship between the United States and east Asia was that it gave each side something that was materially critical. If the economic relationship rested on a structure of shared interests and mutual gain in a world of economic interdependence, then, the optimists argued, it was inherently stable.[14]

As the next chapter will argue, each of these perspectives captured something of the nature of the new economic relationship between east Asia and the United States although the pessimists were undoubtedly correct that it contained significant structural fault-lines. However, even among those who were most pessimistic, none quite foresaw the shape of the crisis of the relationship that developed over Fannie Mae and Freddie Mac in the summer of 2008. Neither had they dwelled on the specific features of domestic American politics out of which the crisis grew. Whilst since the onset of the general financial crisis in the autumn of 2008, many have recognised that the financial flows out of east Asian were the basis of the American subprime boom, what has received far less attention is the degree to which the American state's involvement in the American mortgage market made this specific aspect of east Asian lending to the United States possible and how it produced the consequences that have followed from that one. In crucial ways, the American mortgage market is a political, not financial creation that has long depended on the American state. The American federal state has involved itself in expanding and maintaining home ownership since the early 1930s. By the mid-1970s, the federal government was directly involved in the mortgage market through the Federal Housing Administration (FHA), which provided mortgage insurance to lenders, and indirectly through Fannie Mae and Freddie Mac, which, although private corporations, had to meet policy goals set by the Department of Housing and Urban Development. Since the late 1960s, the American federal government has also made a series of moves to address the legacy of segregation and discrimination against minorities in the mortgage market and expand home ownership among African-American and

Latino households. In providing both direct and indirect material support to lower-income groups mortgage holders, the American government has, in Leonard Seabrooke's words, 'permitted unprecedented levels of state-empowered credit in pursuit of [these households'] life-chances',[15] and in the first decade of this century it encouraged vast international capital flows to that end.

It was the engagement of the American state in the American mortgage market, which meant that other states' central banks were willing to lend directly to Fannie Mae and Freddie Mac even though they were privately-owned corporations. As investors believed that the two corporations were ultimately backed by the American state, whatever official rhetoric to the contrary, Fannie Mae and Freddie Mac were able to issue debt and mortgage-based securities at below market rates of interest. After the fallout of the Asian financial crisis, the Asian central banks proved willing to hold large quantities of the two corporations' bonds and securities as foreign exchange reserves. However, whilst there were good reasons for the east Asian central bank to suppose that any American government would have no choice but to guarantee the corporations' debt, especially once they, as major purchasers of dollar assets, held so much of it, the precise nature of the American state's support for Fannie Mae and Freddie Mac was politically uncertain.

As a consequence of the state's involvement in the mortgage market, the finance of home ownership is more politically contested in the United States than it is in any other rich economy. For much of the past ten years that political contest primarily took place over Fannie Mae and Freddie Mac. From the late 1990s, these corporations grew into huge, highly leveraged entities that dominated the American mortgage market. Their indebtedness, combined with the size of the investment portfolios they accumulated, caused some, including the then Chair of the Federal Reserve Board, Alan Greenspan, to worry that their practices posed a significant risk to the entire American financial system. These concerns were magnified by revelations in 2003 by the Office of Federal Housing Enterprise Oversight (OFHEO), the then federal authority with regulatory responsible for the corporations, that they had systematically engaged in irregular and illegal accounting practices in part to award large executive bonuses. From 2003, the Bush administration, supported by a section of the Republican party in Congress, pushed repeatedly for legislation to put

Fannie Mae and Freddie Mac under a much tighter regulatory regime. The reformers argued that the two corporations were running significant financial risks and that these mattered as much for the future of the American economy as the housing goals Fannie Mae and Freddie Mac were supposedly pursuing. Their opponents wanted to protect the corporations' borrowing, investment portfolios, and corporate reputation in the name of expanding home ownership and affordable housing to minorities. They denied that the two companies were creating a risk either for themselves or the financial system, and attacked those who wanted new regulation as unsympathetic to widening mortgage opportunities to lower-income groups.

In lending to Fannie Mae and Freddie Mac because they believed that their debt was guaranteed by the American state, the east Asian states tied their financial relationship with the United States to the complex domestic politics of home ownership in the United States. Whilst the Bush administration's rescue of Fannie Mae and Freddie Mac in September 2008 did not produce dissent within Congress, the very fact that the rescue was necessary only led credence to the arguments of those who had argued for much of the previous decade that the American state had over-burdened itself in supporting mortgage corporations that precisely because of the institutional political framework in which they operated lacked the incentives to pursue prudent business strategies. Even though the American government had guaranteed the debt held by the east Asian central banks, those central banks were nonetheless left holding the bonds and securities of two mortgage corporations with politically uncertain futures and because of that uncertainty they still wished to rid themselves of their existing assets and refused to resume lending. This part of the economic relationship between the United States and east Asia drew to a close because the political conditions that underpinned it changed, and any analysis of the changes in that the economic relationship wrought by the financial crisis must recognise that.

## Interdependence and its consequences

The nature of the economic relationship between the United States and China that has developed over the past decade, the way it played out through the rescue of Fannie Mae and Freddie Mac and the financial crisis of 2008 raises some important questions about the nature of interdependence in the world today. Scholars have used the term interdependence to capture a range of rather different recent economic, social and political phenomena. Several of these phenomena have frequently been bundled together under the term 'globalisation'. Since the 1990s it has become something of an academic commonplace that globalisation has created an era of interdependence. In this new world, these scholars argued the economic, social and political realms are interdependent and the spatial relations within, and between, each of these realms are not demarcated by state boundaries. What matters for understanding the economic relationship between the United States and China is the way in which actors on each side across the different realms impact on others such that none on either side has autonomy. Put differently, seen in this way, the United States and China exist within a global, or at least heavily internationalised, economic, political and social space beyond the control of either. Within that global space, the ties of interdependence between the two countries are particularly strong because their economic interconnectedness has penetrated so deeply.

From this perspective, there is a clear explanation both of the manner in which the loss of confidence of China's central bank and other state agencies in their American investments in the summer of 2008 helped to precipitate the crisis at Fannie Mae and Freddie Mac and of the response of the American government to that crisis. China's economy was too exposed to the American for the Chinese political leadership not to worry about the fallout of the collapse of the American sub-prime sector and the United States' economy was too dependent on Chinese lending to do anything but assume responsibility for the two mortgage corporations' debts. Economic interdependence determined the outcome and it did so by creating realities that were stronger than any independent political will that could be manifested in either state.

The argument that globalisation has created a new world of interdependence has some important implications. It tends decisively to disconnect the world today from the economic and political past and it tends to diminish the role of the state.[16] The implicit contrast in the thesis that globalisation has created a new world of interdependence, or at least a new kind of interdependence, is with a world in which states mattered more as sites of political agency and identity. The argument takes different forms. Some have argued that states are just able to do less because under conditions of interdependence they have less power than they did and fewer policy options.[17] In a world in which states could do less, new forms of governance, which were more fragmented than anything seen since the creation of modern states, emerged.[18] Others claimed that states are becoming disaggregated. Anne-Marie Slaughter, for example, has argued that different parts of the state have to form their own relations with their counterparts in other states and international agencies and these are more significant to that sub-part of the state than internal state relations.[19] These kinds of approach to interdependence reduced the importance of the political realm. Analytically, they made it less distinctive from the economic, social and cultural realms, and substantively reduced practical and imaginative political possibilities. As Colin Hay has suggested, if the argument that globalisation has created a new kind of interdependence is correct then it is 'more difficult to govern' and 'more difficult for citizens to hold those that would claim to govern to account'.[20]

Casting the economic relationship between the United States and China in such terms, we can construct an argument about the particular consequences of the complexities of interdependence in this instance. First, this is a relationship for which it is hard to find a historical parallel. No other state of any size has developed its economy as rapidly as China by pursuing growth simultaneously through huge export sales into another market and opening up its own domestic markets to large-scale foreign investment. The corollary is that no other developed-country state has, as the United States has done over the past decade, tied so much of its own economy on both the trade and capital side to a particular developing-country economy. There is also not an obvious historical parallel for the interdependencies created by the global market for mortgage-backed securities and the connection this created between domestic housing sectors, matters of international financial regulation, the fiscal soundness of local government operations and pension funds, and growth and recession in economies on the other side of the world. A world in which the American mortgage market was fuelled directly and indirectly more by east Asian foreign exchange reserves than domestic savings deposited in local financial associations was transformative of the material prospects and expectations of many American citizens, the kind of economic choices open to governments on both sides of the Pacific, and the business viability of American and Chinese corporations dependent on cheap short-term credit. Second, this perspective would suggest that as a consequence of the kind and scale of economic interdependence that has emerged, the United States and China have less policy autonomy than they did and that the component parts of each state, particularly the two central banks and Treasuries, have had to work out a relationship with each other that is more significant outcome wise than any they might have with the rest of the policy-making apparatus in Washington and Beijing respectively. Third, this perspective would indicate that the interdependence of the two economies is likely to act as a decisive constraint on the potential for political conflict between the United States and China. Finally, and more broadly, it would stress that the economic relationship between the United States and China is in itself an agent of interdependence. The financial crisis of 2008 that this interdependence helped to precipitate created a huge set of economic and political difficulties for a very large number of states, banks, corporations and public sectors simultaneously. The responses of these actors to the crisis then had direct consequences for others across the world, and the way these actors responded let loose complex distributional issues between states about burden-sharing in dealing with common predicaments.

Nonetheless, the argument that globalisation created a new world of interdependence which has transformed the political world is problematic in several respects. Economic interdependence is simply not a new phenomenon and neither are its political consequences.[21] For example, many of the political problems created by open capital flows between states, for example, played out during the inter-war years in ways that were far more dramatic than the problems generated by the financial liberalisation of the past 30 years.[22] If there is something new in today's world, it has to be that interdependence now takes a different economic form because of the intensity of the mutual relationships and, as a result of that intensity, has sharper political consequences. There are some good reasons to think that the first claim is true. Most fundamentally, there is now far more mobile capital in the world economy and it can be moved far more rapidly between economies than has ever been the case hitherto in periods of significant international economic interdependence.[23] The question is whether the political consequences of this new kind of economic interdependence are a genuinely new phenomenon.

Here the argument that globalisation changed the nature of interdependence turns on the present nature of the state: what it does and does not have the autonomy to do and its internal coherence. In terms of substantive policy-making, the state was rather more robust than the globalisation thesis about interdependence has suggested. Despite financial liberalisation, the growth of enormous foreign exchange markets, the expansion of international trade, the spread of production processes across national economies, and the proliferation of foreign direct investment, states retained considerable power.[24] They were able to use that power to maintain politically distinct national economies.[25] And, it was states themselves that drove financial liberalisation after the end of the Bretton Woods regime.[26] Crucially, much of the comparative empirical evidence about the policies actually pursued by developed- and developing-country states does not support the claim that interdependence had rendered states relatively impotent or condemned them to a narrow range of economic possibilities.[27] Some developing-country states were even able to control short-term capital flows when these were taken by some globalisation scholars to be the juggernaut most weakening the state. Studies of economic decision-making in particular states over the last 30 years strongly suggest that the contingent political judgements of those in government at any particular time matter causally and they have to be understood within domestic political contexts.[28] Even where economic interdependence creates genuine constraints that reduce economic discretion, unless politicians are willing to choose self-destructively, how those politicians themselves perceive interdependence matters. On the one hand, policy-makers can misunderstand it and consequently make misjudgements, either failing to see, or being unwilling to acknowledge constraints that are in fact there. Alternatively, politicians in office can find it useful to present constraints that do not exist to reduce expectations from within their party and their constituents about what they can do with power.[29]

In part those who stressed the state's weakness under the recent form of economic interdependence mistook the nature of the state itself. In doing so they assumed that if the state did not do all those things that western governments had politically chosen to do in the 1930s and 1940s that the state itself was a weaker political actor than hitherto. Yet the state is first and foremost a political entity and cannot be defined by its economic purposes, or indeed any particular set of policy commitments at a given historical moment. As Max Weber explained, the modern state is a site of exclusive authoritative rule by human beings over human beings in a strictly demarcated territorial area, which rests on the application of law and in the final instance the legitimate use of violence.[30] When the state is understood as such a political entity, the question of the relations of parts of the state to sites of international agency or parts of other states appears in a different light. Parts of any state designated to deal with particular policy matters can develop deeper relations with actors beyond that state without the state changing its character. For interdependence to have changed the state it would have to be the case that under the impact of economic integration either political consent to states had diminished and citizens were looking to alternative political associations, or states were unable to exercise coercive power when necessary to sustain their rule, or that international institutions and international organisations had enforceable legal claims within the territory of hitherto sovereign states.[31] Although there are good arguments to be made that some such developments might have occurred in various poor states, not least in Africa,[32] it is difficult to see where any of these phenomenon has occurred in a rich state beyond the purchase of EU law on the EU's member-states and the rules about qualified-majority voting in several policy areas in the EU's Council of Ministers.

Looking at the development of the economic relationship between the United States and China over time, we can see that the state has mattered as a political entity as have the political judgements of those in government. The move by the Nixon administration to open relations with China, without which it would never have been possible for China to pursue export-led growth through American markets and investments, was driven by a geo-political judgement about the balance of power in the cold war and not economic or social forces. When the Chinese government choose to embark on a new approach to development in the late 1970s by opening up the Chinese economy, the Chinese state remained a crucial economic actor, particularly in directing credit towards export sectors. After the Asian financial crisis, the Chinese government took the decision to accumulate large-scale foreign exchange reserves and used them to maintain an extremely tight exchange rate policy designed to prevent the outcomes markets would have produced. Politically, the capacity of the Chinese Communist party to maintain its grip over the Chinese state and the rule of that state over a huge, heterogeneous population spread over a large territory has so far been undimmed either by a deep economic relationship with a state with a very different form of government or the penetration of Chinese society by international social, cultural and technological influences. The fact that a Communist Chinese state has endured has been an important part of what American policy-makers have been responding to in dealing with the economic relationship, just has the fact that China is integrating itself into an international economy and set of international institutions dominated by the United States been a significant part of what Chinese policy-makers have had to deal. Consequently, the economic relationship between the states has at times been politically contested. The Chinese government was internally extremely divided in 1999 about whether to accept the increased economic interdependence that WTO accession brought, and the Clinton administration had to fight Congress to pursue its preferred trade policy towards China. Meanwhile both the United States and China have ferociously guarded their legal sovereignty from various international organisations and the crucial negotiations on China's accession to the WTO were the bilateral ones between the United States and China over permanent normal trade relations between the two states rather than those that produced the final multilateral agreement. Both the state and politics matter in their own terms in understanding how economic interdependence produced the crisis in the summer of 2008.

Interdependence and its consequences have also been much debated over the past few decades by scholars in international relations. Liberals have argued that interdependence, and economic interdependence in particular, reduces the likelihood of conflict between states because it creates shared interests.[33] It also generates strong incentives for them to co-operate. In Robert Keohane's, words: 'As interdependence rises the opportunity costs of not co-ordinating policy increase, compared with the costs of sacrificing autonomy as a consequence of making binding agreements.'[34] According to liberals even the United States cannot escape the reality of interdependence. For John Ikenberry: 'What the dominant state wants from other states grows along with its economic size and degree of interdependence ... It will be necessary for the dominant state to reduce its policy autonomy – and do so in a way that other states find credible.'[35] From this perspective, the economic relationship between the United States and China leaves each state unable to make policy decisions without regard for the other and puts a premium on using international forums to mediate their policy responses to shared problems.

The problem with the liberal argument is that it assumes a natural convergence between the facts of economic interdependence and politics, as if politics falls into whatever shape international economic flows require or would be optimal to sustain interdependence. Yet in reality, interdependence has to be politically managed and domestic politics is an important constraint on the way governments can respond to the policy dilemmas they do indeed, as liberals insist, share with other states. Whatever the overall universal benefits of international trade, and however much nationalist actions against foreign producers can be economically self-defeating, politicians competing for votes can face considerable incentives to respond to the grievances of those producers who are the immediate losers of international economic competition. There is no *a priori* reason to suppose that any set of politicians will put what is economically advantageous, or what makes co-operation with other states easier, above what in domestic politics is electorally necessary or even simply useful. State debt creates another version of the same problem for governments. Under conditions of economic interdependence money can be borrowed internationally, but the taxes that eventually have to pay for it can only be collected domestically. Increasing taxes or interest rates to pay for debt owed to foreigners can at times prove extremely politically difficult, as the political struggles of various indebted developing-country governments, especially in Latin America, have illustrated. Whatever the financial fallout of putting domestic politics before the constraints of interdependence, politicians will sometimes choose to do it.

American domestic politics has frequently been beset by protectionist passions, especially in the Congress, and these have made international trade a serious domestic political problem at one time or other for every American President since Nixon. Both President Clinton and President Bush jnr failed in important parts of their push for more trade liberalisation either because they could not procure fast-track authority from Congress or because Congress refused to ratify the agreements that they did negotiate. The question of trade for American Presidents has long gone beyond the immediate economic question of whether to protect inefficient domestic producers. For example, when, in 2008, Congress rejected the free trade treaty negotiated by the Bush jnr administration with Colombia it was repudiating an agreement that, in opening up previously closed Colombian markets to American exports whilst 90 per cent of Columbian exports already enjoyed free access to the United States, was of significantly more immediate economic benefit to the United States than its trading partner. Trade matters in American domestic politics not just because some of those who lose from it have been politically well organised but in what it appears to represent about the United States' power and general relationships with other states. Many Americans have politically seen the protracted American trade deficit as a symbol of American weakness and the parallel trade surpluses of first Japan and then China as threats to American wealth and power. They have been quick to charge that other states, particularly those in east Asia, have engaged in unfair competition, and they have wanted to tie trade relations with other states to human rights and labour and environmental standards issues.

Just as importantly, policy autonomy can be a domestic political good in itself whatever the international economic rationale for compromising it. Put differently, governments can attach considerable importance for domestic political reasons to creating the perception of policy autonomy for its own sake. Clearly, analytically autonomy and sovereignty are very different concepts. But the fact that politicians in nation-states have long used a language of national independence and self-determination in ways that have run roughshod over the distinction, especially perhaps when it has come to economic matters, has meant that policies which clearly show a government's decision-making to be constrained by external forces, whether those be markets, other states, or international organisations, are often a domestic political risk. During the years of the Bretton Woods international monetary and exchange rate order the levels of economic interdependence between the United States and the western Europe and Japanese economies deepened. Yet as they did so did the constraints on monetary and fiscal policy imposed on American decision-makers by maintaining dollar-gold convertibility. When sustaining that convertibility would have required the Nixon administration to accept a tighter fiscal policy and the American Federal Reserve Board to push interest rates higher, the President and his advisors chose simply to dismantle the foundations of the entire Bretton Woods system. They did so without the semblance of co-operation with other states whose economies would be hurt and who were members of the IMF, which had supposed authority over exchange rates. Asked at the meeting that took the decision to end dollar-gold convertibility about the consequences for the United States' relations with other states for acting unilaterally in the face of what were shared economic difficulties, the then American Treasury Secretary, John Connolly, replied: 'We'll go broke getting their good will. ... Why do we have to be reasonable?.'[36] Forced to choose between the imperatives created on the one side by economic interdependence and multilateral rules and on the other by those generated by economic uncertainty, the desire to avoid macro-economic choices that would hurt the American electorate, and growing protectionist demands in the run-up to the presidential election of 1971, the Nixon administration put domestic politics first.

American Presidents have to manage economic interdependence with China within such domestic political constraints. In several respects, any deep economic relationship with China was always going to create particularly awkward domestic political difficulties for American politicians. China is a Communist regime with which the United States has only had diplomatic relations since 1979 and after Tian'anmen the American government suspended all high-level official meetings and imposed economic sanctions. Prior to China's membership of the WTO, China's most-favoured nation status for trade was subject to annual renewal and Congress tried in the aftermath of Tian'anmen to end it by tying it to China's human rights performance. The sheer speed of China's economic rise after the Asian financial crisis created considerable fear among some Americans. In a very short period of time, China accumulated a large trade surplus with the United States of a kind, and on a scale, that had engendered the Japanese-bashing rhetoric of American politics in the second half of the 1980s. In these circumstances, any American President seen to accept a reduction in policy autonomy for maintaining the economic relationship would run a domestic political risk.

In assuming that economic interdependence reduces the likelihood of conflict between states, liberals also risk paying insufficient to power relations between states in the face of interdependence. In its most basic sense interdependence means that different entities depend on each other. Colin Hay has recently argued that this dependence is best conceived as 'reciprocal causation' such that 'any change in one [entity] will result in a change in all the others'.[37] However, this in itself does not tell us anything about the size of the impact a change in one entity will have on another and whether the impact of a change in one entity will be as significant for the others as for itself or vice versa. Neither does it tell us anything about whether one entity has a greater capacity to withstand change than the others, or whether one entity has the ability to push any of the costs of the interdependence onto others. In the present economic and political world, sharp power relations still exist between states in a situation of economic interdependence. Where there are power relations there is also dependence. The way that dependence shapes the way governments respond to economic interdependence cannot be separated from power relations between states in other realms, especially the security sphere. As noted earlier, in the second half of 1980s the Reagan administration was able to push successive governments in Japan towards macro-economic policies more conducive to American monetary and exchange rates interests than Japanese. It was able to do so in good part because Japan was dependent on the United States for its security. Whatever the mutual ties created by economic interdependence, the United States and China are very far from being equals in any of the economic, diplomatic or military realms. The United States is the dominant power in the world. Its GDP is more than three times than China, its GDP per capita is nearly eight times higher, and its military expenditure is more than seven times greater. The sheer difference in wealth and power between the two states is part of the context in which each deals with interdependence. The Clinton administration was able to impose upon the Chinese terms to accede to the WTO that allow until 2013 any other state to impose unilateral restrictions on any Chinese import if it can show that 'material damage' is being done to its domestic producers. The administration also forced China to reduce tariffs on some agricultural imports into China to virtually zero whilst the Americans, Europeans and Japanese maintain a fiercely protectionist stance on agricultural goods. Power is inherent to the ways in which states deal with their interdependence.

Nowhere is this clearer than in the realm of monetary and exchange rate matters. The United States possesses the premier international currency whilst China maintains restrictions on the convertibility of the yuan on its capital account. Like all other states, except the United States itself, China lives in an economic world in which it needs to earn and to hold large quantities of dollars for various purposes and in which the monetary actions of the American central bank can have a huge impact on its domestic economy. There is no symmetrical dependence of the United States on China, however much the United States borrows from China, because the dollar's position as the dominant currency in international trade, the currency in which oil is transacted, and the primary international reserve currency is unique. Whatever the mutual constraints created by economic interdependence, there are simply ways in which China is acutely constrained by the United States that are not reciprocal, and American Presidents have been willing to use them to American advantage.

Realist international relations' scholars have long believed that the relationship between the interdependence of international economic life and international politics is not as benign as liberals suppose. They argue both that powerful states can engage in conflict, and even war, against a single rival without inflicting significant economic damage on themselves,[38] and that international economic flows create genuine conflicts of interests between states.[39] They also insist that what they see as the anarchic nature of international politics generates specific security problems that exist independently of economic forces, however much what happens in one economy impacts on another.[40] Empirically, they point to the First World War as proof that deep economic interdependence is entirely compatible with intense military conflict between states.[41] For realists, as summarised by Kenneth Waltz, 'interdependence promotes war as well as peace'.[42] Looking at the world today, Waltz has argued that since economic interdependence today co-exists with growing inequality between states, it has actually made international politics more, not less, fraught.[43]

Seen in realist terms, the economic relationship between the United States and China is inherently vexed and the general conflictual relationship between the United States as the world's dominant power and China as the world's rising power will shape the nature of the economic relationship more than the facts of interdependence. Put differently, the American and Chinese governments do not have the incentive to co-operate in the face of their economic interdependence, nor can they afford to put more premium on their shared economic interests than long-term security prospects. For an American realist like John Mearsheimer, the United States faces a threat to its interests in Asia from China's economic rise because that growing wealth will eventually strengthen China's military power. Accordingly, for Mearsheimer, 'the United States has a profound interest in seeing Chinese economic growth slow considerably'.[44]

Whilst realists are correct that there is no necessary relationship between economic interdependence and co-operation, or reduced conflict, between states, they tend to ignore the contingent and specific ways in which interdependence constrains policy choices for states and assume too strict a separation between security matters, international economic issues and domestic politics. The analytical disassociation that realists make neglects even in their own terms the question of how states finance their security policies. In an age of open financial flows, it is very easy for states to borrow money to pay among other things for increased military expenditure not just in private international capital markets but also from other states' central banks. This reality has particular significance in the case of the present interdependence between the United States and China. The American state did borrow significant sums of money from the Chinese state after 2000 and it did so in significant part to finance the war in Iraq. Procuring cheap credit from China allowed the United States to exercise power in part of the world long-considered central to its geo-political and economic interests without asking its own citizens to make an immediate material sacrifice either via increased taxes or higher interest rates to pay for that strategic move. From the American perspective, the safety-check for security on this financial arrangement had to be that China could only end its lending, and thereby require the United States to absorb the financial cost of the war in the short term, by hurting its own economy. Seeing that states still matter as individual actors under conditions of interdependence, as realists do, is not a reason to simplify the complex political conditions under which they act. Since states are first and foremost sites of domestic rule, since they have to legitimate that rule and have come to do so in good part by economic means, and since their ability to deliver prosperity is shaped by the contours of interdependence, they cannot deal with other states without significant regard for the economic relations between them. That economic interdependence does not, and cannot, determine relations between states does not mean that it is not a crucial component of the context in which they interact.

For all their serious differences most approaches to interdependence tend to depoliticise things that are inherently political, including the state itself, and put insufficient weight on domestic politics. By contrast, this book starts from the premise that the political and the contingencies generated by politics matter both domestically and internationally. In placing significant analytical weight on the political, the book argues that the domestic politics of states will change the contours of economic interdependence over time. Economic interdependence is not a natural fact but requires political support, the existence of which is contingent on matters beyond the material realities of interdependence itself. In this case, whilst interdependence was a stabilising dynamic within the relationship between the United States and east Asia, and China in particular, it co-existed with more destabilising political dynamics, leaving the relationship prone to change over time and vulnerable to crisis.

Whilst much of the analysis of consequences of interdependence has been shaped by the academic division between international political economy, international relations, and comparative domestic politics, the nature of the economic relationship between the United States and China as it played out after 2000 demonstrates acutely just how far the facts of economic interdependence, the reality of power relations between states, and the contingencies of domestic politics need to be analysed together. It also demonstrates the importance of looking at the specifics of each of these things before postulating any kind of general claims about economic interdependence or its relationship to international power relations. Whilst much scholarly work about the risks inherent in the economic relationship between east Asia and the United States had focused on the dollar, the actual vulnerability in the relationship that played out in the summer of

2008 arose in significant part out of long-standing political commitments in the United States to the spread of home ownership. Just as potently, the development of the economic relationship between the United States and China and its ramifications shows the importance of in-time analysis. The responses of the east Asian governments to the specific problems of economic interdependence at particular moments changed the economic and political consequences of that interdependence over time and created new power relations in doing so.

## Aims and organisation of the book

This book seeks to explain the origins of the crisis in the economic relationship between the United States and east Asia, and China in particular, in the summer of 2008 around Fannie Mae and Freddie Mac, and to analyse the significance of that crisis in terms of interdependence. It argues that those origins lay in the interaction of some specific features of the international economy that emerged after 2000 and the domestic politics of home ownership in the United States.[45] It examines from a historical perspective the specific features of each that brought the crisis about. What the book does not do is examine the domestic politics behind China's, or any of the other east Asian states', strategic financial decisions during the years leading up to the crisis of summer 2008. Whilst the complexity of this politics explains some of the strategic decisions made by the Chinese leadership about holding dollar assets after the Asian financial crisis, it is not in itself part of the explanation of the specific crisis that developed around Fannie Mae and Freddie Mac.

The book begins by explaining in detail the origins of the post-1998 economic relationship between the United States and east Asia. The first chapter examines the ways in which the east Asian states responded to the Asian financial crisis and how China, in particular, sought to hold the savings from its current account surplus in dollar assets that were either issued, or believed to be guaranteed, by the American government. It proceeds to explain the demand in the United States for Asian capital. It considers the opportunities and risks of this economic relationship from the perspective of both sides and the way those were constructed in the scholarly debate around the relationship.

Chapter 2 examines the politics of home ownership in the United States from the 1930s to the end of the 20th century as the backdrop to the political development of the American mortgage market after 2002. It explains why the American state became so involved in the mortgage market through various federal agencies and Fannie Mae and Freddie Mac. It considers how from the 1960s the American state's involvement with the mortgage market became fused with politically fraught issues around the legacy of segregation, discrimination against African-Americans and minority poverty. Against this backdrop, it explains how the Clinton administration sought to expand home ownership in particular amongst African-Americans and Hispanics, and the consequences of the interaction of this political development with the financial securitisation of mortgages to low-income earners that began in the second half of the 1990s.

Chapter 3 considers the mortgage and financial boom in the United States from 2002 to 2007, the part played in that boom by Fannie Mae and Freddie Mac, and the political battle within Congress over the regulation of these two corporations. It explains why the Bush administration was unable to construct a congressional coalition to pass legislation to establish a new and tougher financial regulator for the two corporations, and it situates that failure in the context of the domestic politics of home ownership in the United States.

Chapter 4 analyses the development of events from the crash of the sub-prime financial bubble in the summer of 2007 through the Federal Reserve Board and Treasury's moves to rescue Fannie Mae and Freddie Mac in 2008 and early 2009. It examines how for the first months after the bubble burst, the east Asian states, and in particular China, provided large sums of capital in the form of bond and equity purchases to various American financial firms, and allowed the two corporations to continue to pump money into the American mortgage market. It explains the implications for China of this continuing transfer of capital to the United States in light of the predicaments it now faced in its economic relationship with the United States and why the Chinese state-investment vehicles became increasingly unwilling through 2008 either to take new stakes in American financial firms or eventually to lend to Fannie Mae and Freddie Mac. The chapter then considers the choices that the conjunction of diminishing benefits of the financial relationship with the east Asian states and the domestic deflation of the mortgage market created for American policy-makers.

The final chapter draws some conclusions. It considers the future of the economic relationship between the United States and China and explains how the interdependencies of the relationship have created fear and the possible implications of this state of affairs. It draws out the importance of politics to understanding the nature of economic interdependence and considers the implications of this for the way we conceptualise and analyse interdependence and international power relations in the present world.

# 2
# Asian Savings and American Borrowing

Economic theory suggests that the capital dynamics of the international economy of the early 21st century should never have happened. That theory says that capital should flow from rich countries to poor ones in search of higher returns. Yet, strikingly, from the late 1990s collectively rich countries became net importers of capital and developing countries became net providers.[1] This phenomenon can be seen in a radical change in the distribution of current account deficits and surpluses. In 1996, the collective current account surpluses of the industrial economies stood at $41.5 billion; by 2000 these economies were running a collective deficit of $331 billion and by 2004 of $400.3 billion. By contrast, the collective current account deficit of developing-country economies stood at $90.4 billion in 1996; by 2000 these economies were running collective surpluses of $131.2 billion in 2000 and $326.4 billion in 2004.[2]

This general picture obscured some more complex particulars. One of the largest richest states in the world – Japan – has been a net exporter of capital since 1981, and another – Germany – had once again become one by 2004. Meanwhile some poorer states have remained net capital importers over the past two decades. At the centre of this odd international economy lay the financial relationship between the United States and east Asia. Much of the net transfer of capital out of developing countries went to the United States. Between 2002 and 2006 gross capital flows into the United States totalled $6.2 trillion.[3] At the beginning of 2006 the US drew in 70 per cent of global capital flows.[4] Just as dramatically, much of the flow of capital came from developing countries and from east Asia and China in particular.

This international economy disproved economic theory in the most fundamental way. The theory was not wrong because circumstances arose in which returns were temporarily higher in developed countries in general, and the United States in particular than they were in developing countries. Indeed returns to capital in the United States were comparatively low. In a study done by Kristin Forbes, the average annual return for the US equity market index in recent years was the lowest in the 52 countries analysed and annual returns in the bond market were 44th out of 47 states.[5] Rather, the theory was wrong because in reducing all economic behaviour to immediate market incentives, it could not account for the range of motivations brought to bear by creditors and debtors in the financial relationship that emerged between the United States on the one side and developing and newly-industrialised countries in east Asia on the other.

The explanation for the apparent oddity of the early 21st-century international economy has been much contested, not least because it has implications for whether the creditor-debtor relationship at its centre was stable and where the burden of adjustment in responding to the problems it has generated should lie. Some, especially in American policy-making circles who have wished to press that burden onto China, have argued that the explanation for the flow of capital lay almost entirely on the savings side in east Asia.[6] Others, who have wished to press at least some of the adjustment onto the United States, have argued that American borrowing imposed an at least partly reluctant burden on the east Asian states to buy dollar assets in an unsustainable manner.[7]

From the first perspective, the United States, as the borrower of last resort, mopped up the consequences of east Asia's deleterious desire to save excessively. Faced with, what the Chairman of the Federal Reserve, Ben Bernanke, described, as 'a global savings glut'[8] the United States' only alternative, Martin Wolf has argued was monetary and fiscal expansion unless the Federal Reserve and the government were willing to accept a recession.[9] This argument, however, is far from persuasive. The United States' current account has been in deficit, except during 1990, since 1982. It began increasing rapidly towards its peak from 1998, a year in which emerging markets and developing countries were also running a collective deficit of nearly 2 per cent of GDP and in which China's trade surplus was less than a third of what it had become by 2007.[10] Put simply, the United States was already a long-term net borrower before Asian savings accelerated.

It is also difficult to reconcile the claim that the United States was a reluctant adjustor to other states' actions and ambitions with the long-standing reality of American monetary power. Since the Nixon administration unilaterally ended gold-dollar convertibility and slapped surcharges on imports in August 1971, American politicians, Treasury officials and the Federal Reserve have not been in the habit of accommodating American macro-economic policy to what other states wished to do. Indeed American policy-makers have not infrequently looked to other states, particularly to Japan, to subvert their monetary interests to those of the United States. Even Martin Wolf, who accepts the central claim of the global saving glut thesis, has to acknowledge that offsetting Asian savings was not 'the explicit intention of US policy-makers' and that American monetary and fiscal policy had the *consequence* of providing demand for Asian capital.[11]

To suggest that the United States increased its borrowing because it was constrained by the east Asian states further ignores the fact that American demand for foreign capital took a specific shape that changed between 2001 and 2007, as the federal government came to borrow rather less and those engaged directly and indirectly with the mortgage market rather more. There is a clear domestic political explanation why the American housing market boomed from 2002, as well as a financial one. Successive American Presidents and Congress wished to increase home ownership and mortgage lending. (This will be discussed in detail in Chapter 4.) The Federal Reserve pursued a monetary policy that allowed, and indeed encouraged, the American housing bubble.[12] It did not do so because it thought it was compelled to act as the reluctant hero of the world economy, forced to sacrifice American medium- to long-term interests to deal with a problem that was not of American making. The Federal Reserve encouraged lending to sustain a housing boom because it wanted to. In Greenspan's own words in his memoirs:

> I was aware that that loosening of mortgage credit terms for subprime borrowers increased financial risk, and that subsided home ownership initiatives distort market outcomes. But I believed

> then, as now, that the benefits of broadened home ownership are worth the risk. Protection of property rights, so critical to a market economy, requires a critical mass of owners to sustain political support.[13]

In sum, the explanation of the financial relationship between the United States and east Asia has to explain both sides' motivations and interests. It matters both why the east Asian states wanted to save and lend so much and why the US wanted to borrow on such a scale. The first phenomena may have made the second possible but that does not make it the primary causal agent.

## Asian savings: The legacy of the Asian financial crisis

The Asian financial crisis of 1997–98 was a crucial turning point for the international economy and the economic and political relationships between east Asia and the rest of the world because it transformed the way that the east Asian governments politically saw monetary and financial issues. During the first half of the 1990s there had been a large outflow of capital from rich states to emerging markets in general and east Asia in particular. Most states in the region had used easy credit and foreign investment to drive growth. This was reflected in the current account deficits of between 4 and 8 per cent run by what would become the four worst afflicted states of the Asian financial crisis – South Korea, Thailand, Indonesia and Malaysia in 1996.[14] The massive capital flight and currency speculation that occurred in 1997–98 and the experience of dealing with the demands of the International Monetary Fund (IMF) and the United States led those governments whose economies and states were hurt by the crisis to see some harsh realities about where the economic policies reflected in these deficits had led.

The Asian financial crisis powerfully demonstrated the economic risk of private borrowing abroad in a foreign currency. Whilst such borrowing had produced strong short-term growth, the price when the value of the currency collapsed and private short-term credit dried up was expensive banking bailouts. The crisis also exposed the international political risk of this kind of borrowing. The dependency that it created on foreign capital had led three states in the region – Indonesia, South Korea and Thailand –into the clutches of the IMF, giving foreigners, and Americans in particular, the opportunity to demand structural reform of their economies in exchange for credit. As Lawrence Summers, the then deputy Treasury secretary in the Clinton administration, said of what the United States gained from the Asian financial crisis: 'the IMF has done more to promote America's trade and investment agenda in East Asia than thirty years of bilateral trade negotiations'.[15] The United States' financial and monetary power had allowed it not just to enforce harsh terms for access to immediate credit through the IMF but also to resist Japan's attempt to establish a regional credit institution in the form of an Asian Monetary Fund that would lend money on less onerous terms. Put in more strategic terms, as Pempel has said, the crisis demonstrated that in a unipolar world, 'the US no longer showed any predisposition to tolerate East Asian models of development when these conflicted with broader US economic or security concerns'.[16] That the Americans expected the east Asian states to accept the constraints on economic development that the IMF conditionality imposed was experienced by the east Asian governments as a public humiliation and produced deep anger across the region.[17]

The events of 1997–8 produced a radical change in economic policy in east Asia, as governments there looked for ways to prevent the possibility of any repetition of the crisis. Collectively, at Japan's initiative, the east Asian states sought to increase regional financial and monetary co-operation, and create an institutional basis for an independent Asian financial institution in the future.[18] Before the crisis there had been very little regional co-operation over financial and currency matters. In December 1997, Japan, China and South Korea agreed to establish a new regional forum, ASEAN plus Three (APT) with the ASEAN states. From 2000 Japan used APT to push the other east Asian states towards an institutional structure that made possible some collective defence of their exchange rates. The Chiang Mai Initiative (CMI) was established in May 2000 to provide emergency liquidity across the region, initially as an expanded ASEAN swap system and bilateral swaps between ASEAN and the three northeast Asian states.[19] In May 2005, the APT states agreed to double the amount of funds available to its members. By May 2008 the total swap size stood at $80 billion.[20] The funds available under the CMI dwarf the IMF quotas of the member-states.[21] Politically, the significance of the establishment of the CMI lay in China's support for the initiative since during the months of the crisis China had opposed the Asian Monetary Fund proposal and supported IMF conditionality.[22]

Meanwhile individual east Asian governments sought to reduce private and state foreign debt and create export-oriented growth. This meant that they had to procure current account surpluses and finance more investment from domestic savings. By the end of 2005, the emerging-market Asian states had a collective surplus of 4 per cent of GDP compared to a collective deficit of 1.7 per cent in 1996.[23] In 2006, the four states that had been worst afflicted during the Asian financial crisis ran current account surpluses ranging from 0.6 to 16 per cent of GDP.[24] In producing these surpluses, the east Asian states rid themselves of a liability that had been central to most of the developing-country and emerging-market financial crises that had occurred since the beginnings of financial liberalisation in the 1970s. The east Asian states wished to escape from the IMF as quickly as possible: Thailand and South Korea repaid their debt early and Indonesia eschewed further credit when its 2000–3 deal expired. Together, these moves reduced the structural risk of a crisis. As a more direct deterrent against the currency speculators, the east Asian governments also began to accumulate large-scale foreign exchange reserves. From December 1999 to March 2007 global foreign exchange reserves increased by $3.5 trillion and $2.36 trillion of those reserves were accumulated in Asia.[25] By the end of 2007, China held more than a trillion dollar of reserves, Japan just short of a trillion, and Korea and Taiwan over $200 billion each.

The consequences of the east Asian states' approach to exchange rate management were potentially self-defeating. Once an increase in exports and a reduction in imports had created a current account surplus, any east Asian government ran the risk that capital inflows would push up the exchange rate and undermine the export competitiveness on which the current account surplus depended, returning the economy to deficit and a subsequent currency crisis. Faced with the risk of currency collapse by this route, the east Asian governments concluded that they also had to limit currency appreciation in the first place. To achieve this, the east Asian states had to accumulate ever more foreign exchange reserves and intervene in the foreign exchange markets when their currencies came under significant upwards pressure.

The most consequential change in economic policy in east Asia after 1997–98 was China's. China was one of the few east Asian states to emerge from the financial crisis relatively unscathed. It was able to maintain the yuan's peg against the dollar as other currencies tumbled by using capital controls, and to contain the consequences of the appreciation of the yuan against the devalued Asian currencies through its export tax rebate system.[26] Nonetheless, the crisis was a severe blow to the Chinese government because it suggested that in a world dominated by American power the east Asian development model was geo-politically and financially problematic. The Chinese leadership was acutely aware that China shared some of the vulnerabilities that had exposed other states in the region, in particular a weak banking system beset with bad loans.[27] Since China was already suffering from illegal capital flight, these problems would be intensified if, as some advocated, it were now to combine a move to open short-term capital flows and a floating currency with its existing openness to foreign direct investment. Seen in these terms, the question for the leadership was how to put in place an economy that would go as far as possible to eliminate any risk of a future financial crisis in which the United States could do to China what via the IMF it had done to other east Asian states. The urgency of resolving this question was intensified by the fact that China's economic development was already vulnerable to a change of approach in Washington. Through the 1990s the Chinese government had looked to export-led growth and encouraged Foreign Direct Investment (FDI) to support that growth. This development strategy depended on access to western markets and that of the United States in particular. China, however, had not been able to put that trading relationship on a secure footing. Having failed in negotiations to get first into General Agreement on Tariffs and Trade (GATT) and then the WTO, it still had to obtain Most Favoured Nation status from the American President on an annual basis. After Tian'anmen this authorisation was a yearly battle.

After the crisis, some within the Chinese government feared that continuing to pursue WTO membership would be a mistake because it would give another stick to a now more powerful United States to beat an Asian state. But Premier Zhu Rongji took a different view and emerged victorious in the internal policy struggle. For Zhu, China simply could not afford to withdraw from the international economy and that meant that it would have to have a more market-oriented economy to satisfy Washington.[28] Zhu's strategic judgement led to two significant changes. Domestically, the Chinese government restructured the economy, most notably opening up the state-owned enterprises to foreign governance strictures and liberalising labour law. Externally, it accepted what the Clinton administration was demanding in a bilateral trade settlement as a prelude to WTO membership. Compared to China's previous negotiating stance, the 1999 bilateral agreement represented a capitulation to the United States.[29] The American Secretary of Agriculture Dan Glickman said of the deal:

> This deal is really a no-brainer. The first question most Americans ask when our trade negotiators bring home a new agreement is: 'What did we give up?' Well, the answer in this case is: 'Absolutely nothing.' Because our market is already open to the Chinese, as evidenced by our current 5-to-1 trade deficit with them. This is not like NAFTA [North American Free Trade Agreement], where we had to give in order to get. In this case, all the concessions are on their side, and all the benefits are on ours.[30]

China then accepted terms of entry to the WTO that were tougher than those agreed with any other state acceding to the organisation since its inception. Until the end of 2013 any other member-state could impose unilateral restrictions on any Chinese import if it could show that 'material damage' was being done to its domestic producers, and until the end of 2008 other member-states could impose unilateral restrictions on Chinese textile via quotas, something that the WTO has never allowed against any other state on any other product. Meanwhile China had to reduce tariffs on some agricultural products to almost zero and eliminate all export subsidies, and, from 2007, make foreign banks eligible to be treated as national Chinese banks.[31]

Zhu's position rested on the judgement that the liberalisation of the domestic economy and WTO membership would produce more rapid growth through exports, and as they did, China would procure the sizeable and stable current account surplus that seemed a necessary condition of financial stability. But, as with the other east Asian states, any such surplus would eventually put upwards pressure on the currency and was likely to provoke American protectionist demands more intensely than elsewhere. What China needed, the government believed, was exchange rate autonomy, both from downward market pressure and upward American political pressure. In putting as much premium as it did on exchange rate autonomy, the Chinese leadership was reacting not just to the Asian financial crisis, but Japan's experience in the second half of the 1980s.[32] Then Washington had forced the Japanese to accept first a rapid appreciation of the yen as part of the 1985 Plaza Accord and then a loose monetary policy to prop the dollar up when the American currency was weakening excessively later in the 1980s. The fallout for Japan after its ensuing asset bubble had burst had been a banking crisis and more than a decade of severe economic difficulty of the kind that would have produced a political disaster in a vastly populated developing country like China.

By the middle of 2005, several things were clear about China's new economic strategy. Even by Asian standards, China was exceptionally focused on savings. The gross national savings rate in China increased by 10 per cent from the late 1990s to 2005.[33] Most of the increase from 2000 came from the corporate sector. By 2006 China's saving's ratio to GDP was just under 60 per cent compared to less than 30 per cent for the other east Asian emerging-market economies collectively.[34] Whilst the Chinese central bank had begun accumulating dollar reserves to try to deter a currency crisis, as the current account surplus had taken off, it had used these savings to purchase huge dollar assets to stop an appreciation of the yuan. Between June 2003 and June 2005, China's official holdings of short- and long-term dollar bonds rose from $255 billion to $527 billion.[35] Once exports were growing significantly more rapidly than imports, the whole structure of the post-1998 development strategy meant these dollar purchases had to continue.[36] For China to change that strategy because of the size of trade imbalance it was creating with the rest of the world and the consequent howls in Washington would have meant sacrificing China's exchange rate autonomy, which the leadership had been determined to protect since the Asian financial crisis. Reflecting that strategic judgement, China's then Premier, Wen Jiabao, warned in November 2004:

> Whether the RMB is revalued or not is an important economic decision. China will never revalue its currency under external pressure. China will consider revaluing its currency only in the right time. If the international society continues to speculate about

RMB appreciation, it is impossible for this policy (revaluation) to be implemented.[37]

From the beginning of 2008 China had both a set of short-term economic interests and some geo-political credibility tied to stopping yuan appreciation. That meant that China would continue to have a huge supply of money available to lend, especially to the United States.

## American borrowing: The budget and current account deficits

The United States' demand for foreign capital over the past decade is reflected in the size of the American current account deficit. In 1997 that deficit had stood at $140 billion. By 2007, it had risen to $788 billion, or 6.5 per cent of GDP.[38] After 2001, the corporate sector, households and the federal government all wanted to borrow and did so in good part from foreign creditors. The budget deficit that accumulated after 2001 represented a significant change in economic policy from the second Clinton administration to the first Bush administration. Very early on in office, President Clinton had concluded that the American federal government, the private sector and households all needed to borrow less because the interest rate cost of financing the trade and budget deficits was hurting the American economy. As he said in his memoirs, 'high interest rates inhibited economic growth and amounted to a huge indirect tax on middle-class Americans who paid more for home mortgages, care payments, and all other purchased financed through borrowing'.[39] Starting from this premise, the Clinton administration moved to eliminate the budget deficit through tax increases and expenditure cuts and to reduce the current account deficit by increasing exports via opening up east Asian markets and Japan's in particular. It was more successful on the first than the second. Having inherited a budget deficit of 4.7 per cent of GDP for 1992, it left a surplus for 2000 of 2.4 per cent. By contrast, the current account deficit swelled from 0.8 per cent to 4.2 per cent over these same years. For its part, the Bush jnr administration returned to deficit financing for each of its eight years in office, with the federal borrowing requirement peaking at 4.8 per cent of GDP in 2003. This borrowing meant that it was possible to pay for a large increase in agricultural subsidies, a significant expansion of Medicare entitlements, and the Iraq war, not only without raising taxes but whilst making two rounds of tax cuts.

The Bush administration was practically able to operate without an interest rate constraint on borrowing because the east Asian states and other foreign investors were willing to lend at a loss. The Clinton administration had seen interest rates as a constraint on American economic policy because they were: discount rates had been 7 per cent at the beginning of 1990 and ranged from 3 to 6.5 per cent during the Clinton years. By contrast, discount rates ranged between 1 and 1.75 per cent from December 2001 to November 2004 and did not rise to 3 per cent until May 2005.[40] Yet the existence of the opportunity that was open to the Bush jnr administration to borrow cheaply cannot be a sufficient explanation for the decisions it made with Congress to do so. Those decisions were politically motivated. There are plausible counter-factual scenarios in which under a Democratic President there would have been no war in Iraq, almost certainly no large tax cuts for the richest Americans, and under that a fiscally conservative Republican President, or Congress, there would have been no increase in entitlement expenditure.

During the same years as the budget deficit reappeared, the American financial sector and American households rapidly increased their borrowing. The pool of American savings could not possibly sustain this leverage. Gross national savings as a proportion of GDP fell from around 18 per cent of GDP in 2000 to around 14 per cent in 2007.[41] The American household net savings rate fell from just over 10 per cent in 1980 to just 0.5 per cent in 2006.[42] As a corollary, American household debt rose as a percentage of disposable income between 2000 and 2006 by nearly 40 per cent.[43] Much of this borrowing went on mortgages: between 2000 and 2005 net borrowing on home mortgages by the household sector rose from $385.7 billion to $1.04 trillion.[44] Meanwhile, the financial sector's net borrowing rose from $793.8 billion in 2000 to $1.762 trillion 2007.[45]

Together, financial sector and household borrowing produced huge American demand for east Asian savings. These savings were lent in several forms that fuelled the mortgage boom. Commercial banks, including China's state-owned commercial banks, bought bonds issued by the financial sector including mortgage lenders. The east Asian central banks lent to Fannie Mae and Freddie Mac by purchasing their bonds and securities. By June 2007, China officially held $376 billion of agency long-term debt, most of which was issued by Fannie Mae and Freddie Mac,[46] and in reality held a lot more,[47] Japan held $229 billion, South Korea $63 billion and Taiwan $55 billion.[48] Commercial banks and the Chinese central bank purchased mortgage-backed securities on which the growth in American mortgage lending depended. These were tradable securities created by financial firms from bundles of mortgages and packaged according to the risk they contained. In June 2007 foreigners held $594 billion worth of mortgage-backed securities.[49] Cumulatively, in June 2007, foreigners held $1.27 trillion of long-term debt securities and $108 billion of short-term debt securities in the mortgage and thrift sector.[50] The supply of credit available from elsewhere to meet the demand for borrowing by the financial sector and households was also indirectly served by Asian savings. Asian lending at low rates of interest to fund the American budget deficit effectively released other investors to lend to corporations in the housing market. As central bank purchases of long-term Treasury drove yields down, private investors looked for higher returns elsewhere and mortgage-backed assets offered them.

## The economic relationship between the United States and east Asia as a changing political problem

For the optimists this vast flow of capital across the Pacific constituted a mutually beneficial and stable international economic order grounded in the particular relationship between the United State and China, what Niall Ferguson and Moritz Schularick have described as 'Chimerica' in which 'west Chimericans' and 'east Chimericans' were two sides of the same economy.[51] From this perspective there was a benign trade-off between the credit at low real interest rates and cheap imports that China provided to the United States and the open markets, foreign direct investment, and competitive exchange rate that the United States provided to China. In a seminal paper, Dooley, Folkerts-Landau and Garber argued that this new international economy was so stable in its structural underpinnings that it could be described as 'Bretton Woods II', at the centre of which stood a pegged *de facto* exchange rate regime anchored by the relationship between the United States and China. This order, they believed, could last for another two decades because China still had around 200 million peasants to integrate into its manufacturing economy and the United States gained structural macro-economic autonomy.[52] Whilst most economists have long argued that large imbalances in current accounts are over time destabilising, the optimists argued that the American imbalance was not a problem. China's dollar earnings on exports to the US poured back into purchase of Treasury bonds and other financial assets. For China this kept the yuan competitive and fuelled American demand for Chinese exports through low American interest rates. Meanwhile Americans did not need to save more and consume less to reduce the current account deficit because the flow of Chinese savings into the American housing market produced, among other things, rising housing prices that allowed American households to use their houses to release cash to finance increased consumption. Since much of this consumption went on imports it created more demand for Chinese exports, setting the whole virtuous circle off again.[53] This relationship, according to the optimists, benefited other states too. 'Chimerica', Ferguson and Schularick argued, generated strong growth, low real interest rates, low inflation, and rising asset prices across the world.

Whilst the optimists recognised that theoretically the east Asian state as creditors had leverage over the United States, they argued that the kind of economic interdependence that existed ensured that the east Asians could not use it without inflicting huge damage upon themselves.[54] In arguing that interdependence radically reduced the policy options on each side, the optimists had a strong case. Perhaps at no point was that made clearer than when South Korea appeared to try to change course. In February 2005, its central bank published a report to the Korean parliament saying that it would diversify the country's foreign exchange reserves. Almost immediately, the dollar dropped below 1,000 against the Korean currency, the won, for the first time in seven years and, more significantly, it also fell against all the major currencies. The Korean central bank quickly retreated and purchased dollars. Three months later, it tried again and the same thing happened: the Korean central bank governor said that Korea would not be buying any more dollars, the dollar fell, and the next day the central bank intervened in the foreign exchange markets to support the dollar.[55] Whatever the burden of the state's dollar assets, the South Koreans could not withdraw their support for the dollar without precipitating a slump in the dollar that was inimical to their interests.

For the pessimists, the economic relationship between the United States and east Asia was far less stable than this liberal optimism about the mutual pay-offs and ties of economic interdependence supposed. Lawrence Summers described the relationship as a 'balance of financial terror' because he foresaw a nightmare scenario for each side if the dollar were to collapse in the foreign exchange markets. In these circumstances China would be left facing a rapid and large appreciation of the yuan with huge consequences for unemployment in the export sector and a massive shock to its banking system given its exposure to dollar assets. For its part, the United States would be unable to service its budget and current account deficits without either a significant increase in interest rates or substantial fiscal retrenchment and a sharp increase in domestic savings, all of which would have deleterious consequences for American growth and employment. Moreover, the consequences on each side of the Pacific of the fallout would reinforce each other and almost certainly produce a global trade recession.

For most of the pessimists, the weakness in the relationship that created the risk of such a crisis developing was the American current account deficit. The former Federal Reserve Chairman, Paul Volcker, insisted that there was simply no historical precedent for a state being able to support a balance of payments deficit the size of the one the United States was running by the middle of the decade. Sooner or later, he stressed, there would be a crisis of confidence in the dollar brought about by the deficit and the Pacific economic relationship would unravel.[56] In a similar vein, Brad Setser and Nouriel Roubini argued in 2005 that the east Asian states would eventually insist on higher interest rates to finance the deficit and that they could do that without precipitating a dollar crisis by slowing their new purchases of dollar assets.[57] Others were sceptical about the argument pushed by Dooley, Folkerts-Landau and Garber that a *de facto* exchange rate system had emerged because they thought that the financial and monetary part of the Pacific economic relationship lacked viable political foundations. Barry Eichengreen argued that the political conditions that underpinned Bretton Woods in the 1950s and

1960s no longer existed and that the east Asian states would not be able to subordinate their individual interests to a collective good, not least because the general relationship the United States has with China is radically different than ones it had one with West Germany and Japan during the Cold War.[58] For their part, Morris Goldstein and Nicholas Lardy argued in 2005 that any suggestion of a new Bretton Woods was 'at variance with Chinese reality' and ignored the developmental costs to China of the specific economic relationship with the United States that had emerged. China, they insisted, could only maintain its support for the dollar at the expense of domestic financial stability, employment, and access to international markets.[59]

The pessimists were correct in arguing that there were various potentially destabilising forces in different aspects of the Pacific economic relationship, and these became more problematic as time passed. Most fundamentally, the east Asian states were by the middle of the decade accumulating ever more dollar reserves at a low rate of return at ever greater currency risk. Whatever the east Asians states did themselves to shore up the dollar, it was a currency losing value. Between 2002 and 2007, the dollar index, which measures the value of the dollar against a weighted basket of the euro, the yen, sterling, the Swiss franc, the Swedish krona and the Canadian dollar, fell by over 36 per cent. Against the euro, the dollar fell by nearly 40 per cent. This currency risk was a particular problem for China. Here, the conjunction of low returns on American assets with the depreciation of the dollar was compounded by domestic inflation. Some estimated that by 2008, China was losing an extraordinary 7 or 8 per cent of GDP a year on its dollar reserves.[60] Meanwhile China's burgeoning trade surplus from 2004 meant that the Chinese government and central bank had to work harder and harder, both politically and financially, to keep the yuan down against the dollar.

Politically, China's trade surplus became an instrument with which others, especially the United States, tried to beat China into accepting a substantial appreciation of the yuan. In July 2005, against a backdrop of protectionist threats from the American Congress, the Chinese government tried to repackage China's exchange rate stance by abandoning the formal peg against the dollar, which it had maintained since 1994, and adopting a managed float against a basket of currencies and conceding a small 2 per cent revaluation against the dollar in doing so. However, even after this move, American pressure did not abate.

Despite the risks the United States ran if China were to change course, the Bush administration and Congress were determined to shift the terms of the implicit bargain in the economic relationship in the United States' favour. In September 2008, shortly after becoming Treasury Secretary, Hank Paulson persuaded the Chinese government to accept an institutionalised framework for discussing exchange rate and trade issues termed the 'Strategic Economic Dialogue'. He aimed to use this framework as a means to get China to concede a meaningful revaluation of the yuan.[61] Six months later, in a clear demonstration of the Bush administration's willingness to use coercion to get China to act, the Commerce department announced that it would apply American anti-subsidy law to imports from China and imposed countervailing duties on some Chinese paper products. This American pressure became increasingly difficult for the Chinese government to contain. In its formal stance, it seemed to give little away, agreeing in May 2007, to increase the band at which the yuan could float around the central parity on a daily basis from 0.3 per cent either way to 0.5 per cent. But in practice the Chinese government had, since Paulson's launch of the Strategic Economic Dialogue, allowed a significant yuan revaluation.[62] From July 2005 to June 2008, the yuan rose by 23 per cent in real terms.[63]

Financially, after 2004, the domestic cost of even capping yuan appreciation rose. By intervening on such a scale in the foreign exchange markets, the central bank created a significant domestic monetary stimulus. The more the Chinese central bank had to sterilise inflows, the more fierce administrative controls it required. This increasingly subjected bank lending, investment approval, and land use to the exchange rate when monetary policy was already in part subordinate to that end.[64] This left China in a rather similar position to Japan in the second half of the 1980s, with an untamed domestic asset price bubble at a moment when an American administration was eschewing any shift in macro-economic policy to maintain the value of the dollar, despite the fact that having exchange rate autonomy to avoid this just kind of problem had been a crucial part of the strategy that Zhu put in place in 1998–9.

Even the trade benefits that China accrued from the international balance of financial terror had diminished by the second half of the decade. American demand for non-oil imports peaked in 2006 and by 2007 less than 20 per cent of China's exports went to the US. In containing the appreciation of the yuan against the dollar as the significance of exports to the US decreased, China risked the yuan substantially appreciating or depreciating against currencies not tied to the dollar. This would have produced either a loss of competitiveness or demands in other countries for action against Chinese exports. By the end of 2007, with the euro rising substantially against the yuan, the EU's rhetoric against China's trade surplus and exchange rate stance was indeed sharpening. As well as the persistent wrath from the United States, the Chinese government was now under a new round of protectionist pressure from those who were responsible for its largest single export market.

The cumulative short-term costs and medium-term risks of China's financial, monetary, exchange rate, and trade relationship with the United States were compounded by the domestic structure of its economy, which produced over-investment in certain sectors and limited domestic demand. Far from looking at a steady path to two decades of rapid growth grounded in a stable international economic order, as Dooley, Folkerts-Landau and Garber argued, China faced by the second part of the decade a potentially very serious set of problems that in significant part structurally arose from the awkward, and at times confrontational, creditor-debtor relationship that it had developed with the United States. Reflecting this reality, in March 2007, Premier Wen Jiaobo declared that China's existing path of development was 'unstable, unbalanced, uncoordinated, and unsustainable'.[65]

Certainly the economic relationship with east Asia caused the American government and central bank far fewer short-term problems than it did China. Far from being constrained in macro-economic policy, the United States enjoyed monetary and fiscal autonomy. The dollar's relative decline was not inflationary and made the cost of servicing American borrowing cheaper. Nonetheless, the United States was running serious medium- to-long term risks in borrowing in the manner in which it was. By becoming significantly indebted to other states, it had given them potential leverage over its foreign policy. Whilst it might be inconceivable that the three east Asian states – Japan, South Korea, and Taiwan – that were dependent on the US for their security would use the credit they supplied to exact foreign policy concessions, the same could not be said for China. Although China had proved willing to purchase the US Treasury bonds sold to finance the war in Iraq, China had very few economic or geo-political existing interests in Iraq and, consequently, that could not be taken as assurance that the Chinese government would permanently separate out short-term economic calculations from its broader foreign policy aspirations. Whilst the Chinese government since the mid-1990s has generally looked to diffuse security tensions with the United States rather than provoke them, China does have a distinct set of military interests and will, the more it prospers materially, have the military capacity to act to advance them.[66] In borrowing from its long-term military rival, the US had simply taken a risk that no previous dominant power had done.

In the short term, precisely because the most pressing problems generated by the Pacific economic relationship lay in China, the continuance of that relationship on its existing terms did not lie in the United States' hands. In benefitting from a relationship that imposed increasing costs on others, the United States endangered the very autonomy that made borrowing from east Asia so attractive. In attempting to push China into a substantial revaluation of the yuan and thus reduce China's trade gains from the relationship, the Bush administration and Congress only intensified the risk they were running in depending on other states being able to contain the political consequences of problems generated by the international economy. If China had conceded on the currency, the whole rationale it had for lending huge amounts of Chinese savings to the United States would have been fundamentally compromised. If China were not acting to stop market pressure forcing the yuan upwards, the United States was likely to have to find itself with private creditors who actually expected a positive real return on the money they lent. This would have meant higher American interest rates unless the government were to check domestic consumer demand, financial sector and household borrowing, and the fiscal deficit.

For both sides the risks involved in the economic relationship were made more complex by other state players in the dollar game, who themselves had to form judgements about whether east Asian support for the dollar was waning. The other big state dollar players were the energy-producing states including Russia. After Vladimir Putin's arrival in power in 2000, the Russian government had moved to accumulate large-scale reserves for some of the same reasons as the east Asian states. At the end of the 1990s Russia had an exchange rate experience as bad as the east Asian states. It had defaulted on its sovereign debt in

August 1998 and then found that the Clinton administration then used access to an IMF loan to restrict its foreign policy options, most notably during the Kosovo war. The rise in the price of oil from 2002, in part the consequence of China and India's rapid growth, allowed Russia, and other energy producers, to build up savings via a current account surplus and then to purchase dollar assets to guard against any repetition of the 1998–9 financial crisis. At the end of 2002, Russia had $27.7 billion in short- and long-term dollar assets; by June 2007, these had increased more than fivefold to $147.6 billion.[67]

Like the east Asian states, the energy-producing states were holding reserves that after 2002 were losing local-currency value. But since the energy-producing states exported far less than the east Asian states to the US beyond oil and were denominating their primary export in a currency that was losing value, they also faced a stronger set of incentives than the east Asians states to change course. In 2006–7, led by Russia, they in part seemed to do so. Between December 2005 and July 2007 Russia's holdings of short-term dollar assets fell from $101.3 billion to $49.9 billion.[68] In May 2007, Kuwait abandoned the dollar peg, which it had run since 2003 as part of a plan to move to a currency union with other Gulf oil-producing states, and fixed the dinar against a basket of currencies. It did so because the Kuwaiti central bank decided that it could no longer contain the inflationary consequences for the domestic economy of the dollar's depreciation.[69] Six months later, the Nigerian finance minister announced a change in legislation to allow the central bank to diversify the country's foreign exchange reserves out of dollars and the Angolan finance minister declared that Angola was considering diversification too. More cautiously, the Saudi central bank declined to match the cut in interest rates made by the Federal Reserve Board in October 2007, despite running a pegged exchange rate policy that implicitly demanded that Saudi monetary policy matched American.[70]

Whilst these moves by the energy-producing states did not precipitate an immediate crisis of the dollar, they did subtly change the substantive terms of the economic relationship between the United States and east Asia. As others turned away from the dollar and the dollar weakened from 2006, the east Asian states were left to look for larger returns to offer a modicum of compensation for their local currency losses. This meant purchasing fewer Treasury bonds and more of the bonds and securities issued by Fannie Mae and Freddie Mac, since the rates of interest on offer from the two mortgage corporations were somewhat higher. The US Treasury's monthly reports on foreign official purchases of dollar securities show the dramatic change that occurred from 2005. In the 12 months through to January 2005, foreign central banks made net purchases of $182 billion of long-term Treasury bonds and notes and $60.3 billion of agency bonds – almost all of which are issued by Fannie Mae and Freddie Mac. In the 12 months through to January 2008, they made net purchases of $44 billion of Treasury bonds and notes and $103.4 billion of agency bonds.[71] Although escaping much public attention and discussion, the increasing willingness of central banks to discriminate between Treasury bonds and other dollar assets opened up new risks for the United States. Henceforth, it could now be left with rising interest rates on Treasury bonds, or those issued by Fannie Mae and Freddie Mac, without the east Asian states having to precipitate a dollar crisis that would because of the constraints of interdependence inflict damage upon themselves. Whilst the relative shift out of Treasury bonds and into Fannie Mae and Freddie Mac's bonds did not create an immediate problem for the United States since the budget deficit had fallen, in view of the two mortgage corporations' continuing credit requirements, any future shift away from the two mortgage corporations' debt back to Treasury bonds would be an entirely different proposition.

In conclusion, the cumulative consequences of the currency risks that the east Asian states were running, once they were holding large reserves of a currency declining in value, and of the interest-rate risks that the United States ran in borrowing from states that had come to incur local-currency losses on their lending, fundamentally changed the nature of the Pacific economic relationship especially that between the United States and China. Mutual interdependence remained a short-term constraint, but it could not mask the increasingly high price China paid for maintaining the *status quo* and the strategic dilemmas for the Chinese leadership that created. Moreover, the very facts of that interdependence meant that the United States could not indefinitely insulate itself from the consequences of these Chinese problems.

# 3
# The Domestic Politics of American Home Ownership

Home ownership has more political significance in the United States than perhaps any other state in the world. This is both because of the sheer scale of the state's involvement in sustaining and expanding home ownership and because the ways in which the federal government has structured that state intervention have been politically contested. For more than 70 years, the American state has supported home ownership institutionally and materially and in doing so has shaped the terms of the mortgage market that makes ownership viable for most households.[1] The federal government during the 1930s created several federal agencies to reconstruct a collapsed mortgage market. One of those agencies, the Federal Housing Administration (FHA) is today the largest insurer of mortgages in the world. A second of those agencies, Fannie Mae, which was established as a federal mortgage association to develop a secondary mortgage market, enjoyed, as the privatised corporation it became for 40 years, privileged access to Treasury and Federal Reserve support and remained subject to a congressional charter that required it to meet public policy goals set by the federal government. Since September 2008 it is back under direct state control. Over an even longer period, the American state has supported home ownership through the federal tax code. Since federal income tax was first introduced in 1913, interest payments on mortgages have been tax deductible. When legislation in 1986 eliminated all other interest-related personal deductions, those for mortgages and home equity loans remained in place. As Leonard Seabrooke has argued, despite a common perception that the United States has a minimalist state as far as its domestic economy is concerned, it has when it comes to home ownership a very interventionist one.[2]

In most state interventions the question of who benefits most from the deployment of the state's resources is likely to become a contested political issue because the state collects revenue from all taxpayers and frequently distributes its expenditure selectively to some of them. In the case of the American state's provision of financial support for home ownership, the distribution of material benefits has at times been particularly politically charged because for more than three decades one group of citizens, African-Americans, were effectively excluded from receiving the material resources on general offer. Once, in the late 1960s, such discrimination was legally prohibited, the American state became involved in efforts to reverse its legacy on social patterns of home ownership. This produced a new set of contested political issues about the financial consequences of the mortgage lending that subsequently ensued. American Presidents and Congress have long used the American state systematically to support home ownership but they have created various political problem for themselves in doing so, the consequences of which have unfolded in complex ways over time.

## The American state and home ownership

The present-day politics of American home ownership began in the 1930s during the banking crisis precipitated by the international economic collapse that followed the 1929 Wall Street crash. That crisis led to the failure of a third of the country's banks and savings and loan associations. For much of the previous decade the United States had enjoyed a housing boom with total residential mortgage debt tripling between 1920 and 1930.[3] The mortgage market that supported this borrowing has been dominated by local savings and loan associations. These provided mortgages on tough terms, making loans for just five to ten years at an adjustable rate of interest for only 50 per cent of the value of a property. If a household could not get a new loan at the end of the fixed-term contract, it had to repay the existing balance.[4] The interest rates the savings and loan associations charged to mortgage holders were higher than those available to many other borrowers. Whilst the spread between mortgage interest rate and high-grade corporate bonds was about 50 points in the 1980s, in the 1920s it stood at an average of around 200 points.[5] As there were no national mortgage lenders, interest rate costs were also variable across the country. This restricted mortgage market limited home ownership to the better off. Before the 1929 economic crash less than half of American households owned the property in which they lived.

The crash had several lethal consequences for American mortgage holders and lenders. Whilst unemployment soared leaving many households with much reduced income, banks and savings and loan associations, facing an accumulation of bad debt, moved to call in loans. The banks and savings and loan associations then foreclosed on those households that could not repay. Between 1931 and 1935 there were 250,00 foreclosures a year, which meant that 10 per cent of home owners lost their houses.[6] This drastic reduction in the supply of mortgage loans did not return the banks and savings and loan associations to solvency. With housing prices in the first half of the 1930s falling 50 per cent from their peak, foreclosures did not recover the money these financial corporations had lent.

At the beginning of the 1930s economic crisis, the American federal state had virtually no existing legal, material or financial capacity to act. Constitutionally, land use for housing was a state matter and savings and loan associations were regulated by individual states, and the states lacked the resources to deal with what was a national problem. Whilst the push for more general federal intervention in much of the domestic economy came from the Roosevelt administration, it was President Hoover, in the final year of his administration, who first decided to involve the federal government in the mortgage crisis. The Emergency Relief and Construction Act of 1932 created the Reconstruction Finance Corporation (RFC) as an independent federal agency. The RFC was mandated to provide both aid to state and local governments and credit to banks holding bad loans, including mortgage loans and to corporations providing housing for low-income households. In the same year Congress passed the Federal Home Loan Bank Act. This legislation established a Federal Home Loan Banking system, which created 12 regional, federally-chartered Federal Home Loan banks out of insolvent savings and loan associations and mutual savings banks. These new banks then lent to financial corporations who were engaged in mortgage lending and were members of the Federal Home Loan Banking system.

The federal housing legislation of 1932 had little immediate impact on the mortgage market.[7] When Franklin Roosevelt entered the White

House nearly half of the country's mortgages were in default and most banks were shut down leaving many bank accounts frozen. One month into his presidency, Roosevelt told Congress that it was federal policy to protect home ownership.[8] Over the next year his new administration refinanced and reorganised the RFC and pushed through Congress an array of legislation that created more federal agencies to support home ownership. These were designed both to try to resolve the immediate crisis and to put in place an institutional financial structure to prevent a further failure of the mortgage market. On the first, the Roosevelt administration looked to supply new credit directly and indirectly. The Emergency Farm Mortgage Act, passed by Congress in May 1933, created the Farm Credit System as a set of co-operative lending institutions to provide and restructure loans for farm households. The Homeowners' Refinancing Act, passed in June 1933, created the Home Owners' Loan Corporation (HOLC). The HOLC issued bonds supported by the Treasury and used the funds to buy defaulted mortgages in order to restructure them into long-term loans at a fixed rate of interest. In its first year, it restructured around one million loans. Between July 1933 and July 1935 the HOLC made loans to 10 per cent of all owner-occupied, non-farm households.[9] It stopped new lending in 1936 because it had disposed of all the capital available to it under the terms of the legislation. The National Housing Act, passed in 1934, created the Federal Housing Administration to provide federally-guaranteed insurance for investors to buy HOLC-restructured loans. Whilst these moves channelled federal resources directly to lenders and borrowers, the Roosevelt administration also acted to recreate incentives for savers to deposit their surplus cash in private financial corporations in order to increase the supply of capital for mortgage lenders. The Glass-Steagall Act, passed in 1933, established the Federal Deposit Insurance Corporation, which created deposit insurance for commercial banks, and the National Housing Act, passed in 1934, created the Federal Savings and Loan Insurance Corporation to do the same for savings and loan associations.

On the second, the Roosevelt administration and Congress moved to reduce the long-term cost of borrowing for mortgage holders. The HOLC restructured existing loans into a new kind of mortgage. This came at a fixed interest rate, required a small down-payment, and offered a longer maturity. Such a loan became the norm for American mortgages for the next 40 years, until the beginnings of sub-prime lending. Meanwhile, the National Housing Act of 1934 authorised the FHA to establish a federal mortgage corporation that could purchase FHA-guaranteed mortgages from private lenders and so create a secondary mortgage market. In February 1938, the FHA chartered Fannie Mae, known formally as the Federal National Mortgage Association, as a federal agency to meet this remit. The Roosevelt administration wanted Fannie Mae to create a *de facto* national mortgage market that could transcend the variable willingness of local creditors to lend for housing purposes. As a federal agency, Fannie Mae borrowed in markets where there was more credit available and lent where there was less, and it was authorised to issue bonds, which were backed by the government. By having Fannie Mae borrow in private markets from banks and insurance companies, the Roosevelt administration increased the amount of capital available for mortgage lending, when that had previously been constrained by the deposits accumulated by banks and savings and loan associations. It also enhanced the attractiveness of FHA-guaranteed loans to lenders by making them more liquid.[10] During the Second World War, the Roosevelt administration extended the reach of the American state in the mortgage market further. The 1944 Servicemen's Readjustment Act introduced a new class of mortgage loans for returning veterans. These loans required no down-payment, were guaranteed by what was then called the Veterans Administration and is now the Department of Veteran Affairs, and could be purchased by Fannie Mae.

The federal agencies founded during the New Deal and war effectively created state-insured investment for mortgage lenders.[11] Protected as they were by the American state, financial corporations were able to make more loans for home purchases at lower rates of interest than they would have done if they had operated according to the incentives created by the supply and demand dynamics of the mortgage market itself. In their cumulative mandates these federal agencies established the financial basis for a large post-war expansion of home ownership. The rate of American home ownership, which had fallen from 47.8 to 43.6 per cent between 1930 and 1940, rose to 55 per cent in 1950 and to 61.9 per cent in 1960.[12]

However, by the middle of the 1960s, the expansion of home ownership had stalled. This was in part because under the somewhat more inflationary economic conditions of the 1960s the particular structure of the American mortgage market that federal agencies had shaped produced a diminishing pool of capital for home lending despite the incentives generated by federal support for selling mortgages over making other forms of loans. Between July 1963 and April 1969 the Federal Reserve Board raised the discount rate from 3 per cent to 6 per cent to try to combat the inflationary pressure in the economy. Mortgage creditors were left having to offer higher rates on deposits than the fixed rate at which they were lending to their existing customers. As alternative savings vehicles became more attractive, they were also hampered by the restrictions that federal and state legislation placed on the interest return from deposits in bank and savings and loan associations. In 1966, a mini-crisis ensued when interest rates on short-term deposits with mortgage lenders fell below interest rates on short-term Treasury bonds, causing deposits to flow out of savings and loan funds and into Treasury bonds. The disjuncture between the price of the capital that lenders procured and that at which they made loans produced liquidity problems and a significant number of lenders became insolvent.[13] Meanwhile, potential new mortgage holders had to accept a higher fixed rate for a loan than that which had been available for the previous 30 years, hitting the demand for mortgages as the capacity for new supply was diminished.

Although the federal government had the ability to boost liquidity in the market through Fannie Mae, the deterioration in the fiscal balance produced by President Johnson and Congress' desire to fund the Vietnam war, the Great Society and the race to the moon without raising taxes made moves to allow Fannie Mae to increase its borrowing an unattractive proposition. Indeed, to reduce the fiscal pressure, the Johnson administration wanted to take Fannie Mae's liabilities off the federal budget. The practical question was how it could do this without entirely withdrawing the American state from the secondary mortgage sector and, therefore, leaving home ownership to the mercy of market outcomes at a time when the market disincentive to lend for mortgages was strong. The Johnson administration solved the dilemma by splitting Fannie Mae into two. It established the Government National Mortgage Association, which became known as Ginnie Mae, as a new federal agency to purchase FHA-backed and Veteran Affairs-guaranteed loans, and it reinvented Fannie Mae as a privately-owned corporation to buy non-government backed mortgages and raise additional funds for mortgage lending by issuing mortgage-backed securities supported by its loan book. Whilst the new Fannie Mae was shareholder owned, it retained much of its old congressional charter, which had been formalised in 1954. The charter prescribed several public purposes to the corporation: to provide stability in the secondary market for residential mortgages; to respond to the incentives of the private capital market; to increase the liquidity of the mortgage market and capital markets that provided capital for mortgage lending; to promote access to mortgage credit throughout the country, including central cities, rural areas and underserved areas; and to manage and liquidate the existing federally-held mortgage portfolio.[14] To achieve these ends, the administration gave Fannie Mae continued access to the material resources of the state and made it subject to some political control. It was exempt from all local and state taxes except those on property and also from the Securities and Exchange Commission's usual securities registration and reporting requirements for public companies. The Treasury had the discretionary authority to purchase up to $2.25 billion of Fannie Mae's obligations and the Federal Reserve could support its debt too. However, what was left unclear was whether the American state stood behind Fannie Mae's debt, an issue that would later come to have huge consequences. Fannie Mae's charter denied that there was any longer any federal guarantee of the corporation's borrowing. Yet if Fannie Mae's creditors took that proclamation at face value there was no reason for them to lend to the corporation at below market rates, as the Johnson administration appeared to expect them to continue to do. By contrast, the American state's continuing political engagement with Fannie Mae was less ambiguous. Although a private corporation, Fannie Mae could not operate independently of the federal government's home ownership policies. The President could appoint five members of the corporation's board and Fannie Mae was subject to oversight from the Department of Housing and Urban Development and not the regulatory authority of any of those federal financial agencies that supervised American banks, savings and loan associations, and other financial corporations.[15]

The federal government's continuing engagement with the secondary mortgage market intensified when, in 1970, Nixon and Congress created a second congressionally-chartered, private mortgage corporation, Freddie Mac, known formally as the Federal Home Loan Mortgage

Corporation. Freddie Mac operated on the same terms as Fannie Mae. By providing competition for Fannie Mae, the Nixon administration and Congress hoped to drive mortgage interest rates down once again. During the 1970s, the two corporations began to push the mortgage market towards securitisation and the generation of mortgage-backed securities. These provided an income stream for those who held them and made it possible for creditors who packaged loans up and sold them as securities to recuperate the money and make more loans.

Nonetheless, the structural problem of the American mortgage market that had begun in the 1960s remained in place. As interest rates continued to rise, culminating in a discount rate of 14 per cent in 1981, and alternative savings vehicles continued to offer higher returns, savings and loan associations persistently struggled to attract the deposits they needed to make more loans. Without this primary lending, Fannie Mae and Freddie Mac were not a solution. In response, first the Carter and then the Reagan administration, with support from both parties in Congress, moved to liberalise federal rules on lending and savings and the general operation of some financial corporations. The 1980 Depository Institutions Deregulation and Monetary Control Act and the 1982 Garn-St Germain Depository Institutions Act lifted many regulations on savings and loan associations, allowing them, amongst other things, to offer higher interest rates on deposits, to borrow money from the Federal Reserve, to lend more, and generally to act more like banks.

Whilst these legislative changes increased mortgage lending, they also paved the way for the American savings and loan crisis of the 1980s. The reckless lending of many deregulated associations, and the fraud committed by some, produced widespread insolvency in the sector.[16] As in the 1930s, the federal government intervened to protect the mortgage and savings markets from collapse. Between 1986 and 1989 the Federal Savings and Loan Insurance Corporation paid out on deposits on nearly 300 savings and loan associations before exhausting its resources. In 1989, the Bush snr administration and the Democrat-controlled Congress created the Resolution Trust Corporation as a government-owned company funded by taxes to take over responsibility for the bailout as part of the Financial Institutions Reform, Recovery and Enforcement Act, which was introduced to reform the savings and loan sector. The Resolution Trust Corporation closed and paid out on over 700 more associations. This federal intervention cost the American state at least $124 billion and contributed to a rise in the federal budget deficit from just over 3 per cent of GDP in 1989 to nearly 6 per cent in 1992.[17]

In sum, from the 1930s to the 1980s the American federal government used the material and institutional resources of the American state to support home ownership. It rescued and reconstructed the mortgage market on a grand scale in the 1930s, intervened to try to reduce the cost of borrowing and increase the supply of credit during the 1960s and 1970s, and assumed the liabilities of a large number of mortgage lenders during the 1980s. This engagement of the American state in the mortgage market was sustained regardless of which party was in power in the White House or Congress. It reflected a bipartisan consensus about the political value of home ownership and the need to provide material resources to defend and advance that value.

## The social composition of home ownership

Yet underneath this bipartisan consensus lay an acutely charged political problem. From the start of the spread of home ownership during the first decades of the 20th century, discrimination against African-Americans was common practice amongst private lenders.[18] Crucially, the arrival of the federal government in the mortgage market in the 1930s intensified rather than eliminated that phenomenon. Put bluntly, the federal institutions created in the 1930s operated to support for home ownership for white Americans and not for African-Americans. The FHA and the HOLC encouraged white flight out of the cities into the suburbs and left the inner cities with virtually no federal material support for ownership. In 1935 the Federal Home Loan Bank Board asked the HOLC to draw up what it termed 'residential security maps' for 239 cities.[19] These maps turned inner-city neighbourhoods with African-American residents in into credit risks, a practice that came to be called 'redlining'. Under these maps, half of Detroit's districts and one-third of Chicago's were ineligible for FHA-insured loans.[20] Redlined maps ensured that FHA-insurance was offered almost exclusively on mortgages to buy houses in new suburbs, which the FHA wanted to make and keep racially segregated. The 1938 FHA underwriting manual pronounced: 'if a neighbourhood is to retain stability, it is necessary that properties shall continue to be occupied by the same social and racial classes'.[21] The same manual recommended the use of restrictive convents on property to insure against what it deemed 'inharmonious social groups' living in the same residential area.[22] In this segregationist spirit, the HOLC would not allow African-Americans to buy the foreclosed homes it acquired in white neighbourhoods.[23] The political consequences of this systematic discrimination by the New Deal federal housing agencies were compounded because of other New Deal legislation. The National Labour Relations Act and the Social Security Act, which created union rights and benefits for the unemployed and the retired, had the *de facto* effect of excluding probably two-thirds of African-Americans from their provisions because they left farm workers and those in domestic service, in which sectors a disproportionate number of African-Americans worked, ineligible for coverage.[24]

After the Second World War, the operation of the Veterans Administration loan programme had the same discriminatory and segregationist effects. Mortgage credit backed by the federal government continued to go predominantly to the white suburbs. Even after the Supreme Court in 1948 decided in Shelley versus Kraemer that the Missouri Supreme Court had acted unconstitutionally when it had enforced a restrictive covenant on an African-American family who had purchased a house under such an agreement in St Louis, *de facto* federal support for racial discrimination and segregation continued. Although the FHA did accept after 1948 that it could not use the racial composition of a neighbourhood to determine eligibility for insurance, it did not put any restrictions on discrimination by lenders selling FHA-insured mortgages. Since most private lenders would not lend to African-American households wanting to buy a house in white neighbourhoods, the theoretical availability of FHA-insurance for such a purchase was irrelevant.[25] In total, between 1946 and 1959 perhaps less than 2 per cent of the housing financed with one form or another of federal mortgage assistance was available to African-Americans.[26]

As the post-war civil rights movements gathered political strength, these federal practices came under increasing political attack. The 1959 Commission on Civil Rights declared that 'housing ... seems to be the one commodity in the American market that is not freely available on an equal basis to everybody who can afford it'.[27] The 1961 Commission report devoted an entire volume to the housing issue and placed responsibility for discrimination in access to home ownership firmly on the New Deal federal agencies:

> The Federal Government has been without question the major force in the expansion of the housing and home finance industries. ... But the benefits of these governmental activities have not been available to the American people on an equal opportunity basis ... Of the many federal agencies concerned with housing and home mortgage credit, none has attempted to exert more than a semblance of its authority to secure equal access to the housing benefits it administers, nor to insure equal treatment from the mortgage lenders it supports and supervises. Many have taken no action whatever. And neither the President nor Congress has yet provided the necessary leadership.[28]

However, successive Presidents were cautious in responding to African-American grievances. Although President Kennedy issued an executive order in 1962 that required the FHA and Veterans Administration to insure in only equal-opportunity lending, he eschewed decisive legislative action to reform the federal agencies as for most of his time in office did Lyndon Johnson. However, in pushing the 1968 Civil Rights Act, Johnson changed course and tried to make the federal government an active political agent in procuring more African-American home ownership. The Fair Housing Act, which was title VIII of the 1968 Civil Rights Act, prohibited discrimination in housing, including mortgage lending. The 1968 Housing and Urban Development Act involved the American state far further in the problem and committed new federal money to socially spreading home ownership. Section 235 of that act created subsidised lending for some low- and moderate-income households with the aim that much of the money should go to African-American families. This federal programme provided for a nominal down-payment, FHA insurance, and either interest payments of no more than 1 per cent of the value of the loan or no more than 20 per cent of family income. Between January 1969 and January 1973 about 400,000 loans were made under the scheme.[29] This federal intervention, however, soon hit difficulties. The FHA mismanaged the programme and the lending led to a large number of defaults. In 1972 the Office of Management and Budget warned that the fiscal costs were out of control, and in January

1973 Nixon suspended section 235. Whilst a more modest programme was later reinstated, it had very little impact on the social composition of home ownership and most African-American holders remained renters.

After this failure, Presidents and Congress preferred for the next 20 years to use civil law, rather than create material incentives through the state, to try to get private creditors to lend to minorities, and African-Americans in particular. In 1974 Congress passed the Equal Credit Opportunity Act, which created a civil liability for creditors whom were found guilty of discrimination on basis of race, sex, national origin, marital status or age. In 1975, it passed the Home Mortgage Disclosure Act, which made public data on the particular lending done by individual financial institutions. Most significantly, in 1977, it passed the Community Reinvestment Act (CRA). None of the earlier legislation had created much enforcement capacity for the state. By contrast, the CRA required all the federal financial supervision agencies – the Board of the Federal Reserve System, Comptroller of the Currency, the Federal Deposit Insurance Corporation and the Office of Thrift Supervision – to mandate the individual financial institutions for which they were responsible to lend to low-income areas and neighbourhoods and gave them the authority to stop any expansion or merger of an institution that was not compliant. Only in the aftermath of the savings and loan crisis did American politicians return to more interventionist solutions. On the initiative of Democrats in Congress, the Financial Institutions, Recovery and Enforcement Act established a state-backed Affordable Housing programme for low-income groups.[30]

Whilst overt discrimination declined in the wake of these legislative changes of the 1970s, the impact on the overall rate of home ownership and its social composition was largely static for three decades. From the mid-1960s to the mid-1990s, home ownership increased only slightly. At the beginning of 1965 home ownership was 62.9 per cent; at the beginning of 1975, it was 64.4, at the beginning of 1985 it was 64.1, and at the beginning of 1995 it was 64.2.[31] Meanwhile, the long-standing privileged position of whites over African-Americans in the housing market was increasingly matched by a similar mismatch between whites and Hispanics, as the American Hispanic population grew. US Census data shows that in 1994 the home ownership rate among whites was 70 per cent whilst among Hispanics it was 41 per cent and among African-Americans 42 per cent. Whatever legal protection for minorities existed after 1968, increasing the number of minority home owners required new lending and borrowing and the savings and loans crisis had hurt the supply of new mortgages whilst the high interest rates of the late 1970s and 1980s curtailed demand. Since many minority households had low incomes, they were not eligible for most of the loans that were available under the market conditions of these years. The conjunction of the legacy of racial segregation and discrimination in mortgage lending that had left a disproportionately high number of African-Americans in decaying inner cities, the effective inability of those who had been excluded from home ownership to pass capital to their children, and the continuing income inequality between whites and other groups meant that any substantial change in the social composition of ownership had to mean more lending to those with low income and few, if any, assets.

## The Clinton administration and home ownership

Against this economic and political backdrop, the Clinton administration embarked upon a new federal effort to expand home ownership and minority home ownership in particular. In 1994 it announced that it aimed to achieve an ownership rate of 67.5 per cent by the year 2000.[32] However, it did not want to commit more of the material resources of the American state to realise that end, particularly since it was determined to reduce the federal budget deficit. Consequently, this aspiration had to rely on encouraging creditors in the private mortgage market to lend to households whom had hitherto been excluded from loans. Unlike in the 1970s and 1980s, there was an opportunity for realising such an approach. By the time Clinton had taken office, some private mortgage lenders were indeed looking for new kinds of clients and wished to engage in what came to be called 'sub-prime lending'. Whilst its definition has become contested since it proved catastrophic for the international financial system, sub-prime lending generally entailed making loans to customers whom until the 1990s would have been deemed non-creditworthy because of their income, employment status, or past credit history. Sub-prime loans came with higher interest payments than the conventional, 30-year, amortised (scheduled payments covering principal and interest) loans that had dominated the American mortgage market since the sector's reconstruction in the 1930s. Sub-prime lending had been made legal by the 1980 Depository Institutions Deregulation and Monetary Control Act, which eliminated federal usury restrictions and led the way to states liberalising their interest-rate rules too. The Alternative Mortgage Transaction Parity Act, which Congress passed in 1982, then allowed savings and loan associations and banks to make available a new range of mortgages under different terms than conventional loans.

Sub-prime lending took off in the mid-1990s with sub-prime loans, growing from $65 billion in 1995 to $138 billion in 2000.[33] Much of this lending was undertaken by new creditors who either set themselves up as specialist companies, or were established as separate units by existing banks. The growth of sub-prime lending was fuelled by the increasing securitisation of mortgages that had begun with Fannie Mae and Freddie Mac's activities during the 1970s and had grown in the aftermath of the savings and loan crisis. By the late 1990s, securitisation had created a far greater pool of capital for mortgage lending than deposits and the funds available from financial institutions from which Fannie Mae and Freddie Mac could borrow. That pool included international capital markets.[34] By 1998, 55 per cent of sub-prime loans were securitised compared to 28 per cent in 1995, the last year before sub-prime lending accelerated.[35]

Wanting more private capital to be made available, the Clinton administration did nothing to discourage the securitisation of mortgages, despite the warnings by some that the financial derivatives that the process was generating were risky. Indeed the Clinton administration, supported by the Federal Reserve under Alan Greenspan's chairmanship, adopted a hands-off approach to the whole operation of the financial markets, as financial derivatives in the mortgage and other sectors expanded. Whilst the Democrats still controlled Congress, Edward Markey, a representative in the House from Massachusetts, had the sub-committee he chaired commission a report from the Government Accounting Office on financial derivatives. This report was published in May 1994. It recommended a new regulatory framework for derivatives and counselled that the absence of one might threaten the safety and soundness of the American financial system.[36] Whilst Markey responded to the report by introducing a bill to establish regulation over derivatives, Clinton's Treasury under-Secretary, Frank Newman, was dismissive:

> I don't know any of any new authority that bank regulators feel they need. It's a risk that needs to be looked at. But I don't think anyone including the Government Accounting Office, is portraying this as some imminent likely danger.[37]

Without White House support, Markey's bill went nowhere, as did legislation he subsequently introduced in 1995 and 1999 when the Republicans controlled both houses of Congress. In 1997 the Commodity Futures Trading Commission, a federal agency created by Congress in 1974 to regulate commodity futures and options markets, started looking, under Brooksley Born's chairpersonship, at whether new financial derivatives, primarily swaps that were not covered by the Commission's existing regulatory rules, should be regulated. The Treasury responded by saying that just discussing the possibility of new restrictions threatened the derivatives market. In May 1998, Robert Rubin, Clinton's Treasury Secretary, and Alan Greenspan asked Congress to prevent Born from acting on swaps until more senior regulators had engaged with the issue and Congress froze the Commodity Futures Trading Commission's competence to consider swaps for six months. After losing the political battle that ensued, Born resigned. In November 1999, the Treasury and Greenspan recommended that Congress permanently exclude the Commission from any regulatory authority over derivatives.[38] As his administration was coming to an end in December 2000, President Clinton signed into law the Commodity Futures Modernisation Act, which ensured that products offered by banking institutions would not be regulated as futures contracts and hence would not fall under the Commission's legal remit.

Meanwhile, in regard to the primary mortgage market, the Clinton administration directly pushed banks and mortgage corporations to lend more to low-income earners through new legislation and changes to existing laws and rules. It opened up FHA-insured loan requirements to make them easier for low-income groups to procure. It encouraged passage of the Riegle Community Development Financial Institutions Act of 1994, which created a Community Development Financial Institutions Fund within the Treasury to enhance the capacity of financial institutions to provide credit to underserved populations and communities. The following year the administration pushed through significant revisions to the Community Reinvestment Act.[39] These required banks and other financial corporations to break down lending data by neighbourhood and income, strengthened the capacity of the federal regulatory agencies to enforce CRA requirements, and allowed community groups a formal role in monitoring banks' CRA compliance. In 1998, the Clinton administration insisted that the President would veto what eventually became the Financial Services Modernisation Act, which repealed the Glass-Steagall Act that had stood since the New Deal and forbade mergers between commercial and investment banks, unless the bill maintained the entirety of the existing rules of the Community Reinvestment Act, despite its strong active support for the bill's primary purposes. Since its main Republican sponsor in the Senate, Phil Gramm, did not want to pass anything that extended the application of the CRA, the bill stalled until a compromise was reached that upheld most of the CRA but exempted smaller banks with good CRA track records from frequent review.[40]

Perhaps most consequentially, the Clinton administration in its second term drove Fannie Mae and Freddie Mac towards sub-prime lending and to purchase sub-prime mortgage-backed securities. Before the Clinton administration arrived in office, Congress had already made changes to Fannie Mae and Freddie Mac's charters in order to involve the two mortgage corporations more in the secondary market for loans for low-income earners. In 1992 it had passed the Federal Housing Enterprises Financial Safety and Soundness Act. This bill was sponsored in the Senate by Dan Riegle, the Democrat Chair of the Senate Banking, Housing and Urban Affairs Committee and in the House by a Democrat representative, Henry Gonzales, and a Republican, Chalmers Wylie.[41] In the Senate the bill passed 77 to 19 with the no votes all coming from Republican members. The act amended the charters of Fannie Mae and Freddie Mac to create statutory mandated national targets for the two corporations to achieve in the provision of housing for each of low- and moderate-income groups and low-income families in low-income areas and very low-income families termed 'special affordable housing', and a separate geographically-based target for cities, rural areas and underserved communities. Henceforth, the Department of Housing and Urban Development would set and enforce a minimal percentage target for the proportion of mortgages made to each group that Fannie Mae and Freddie Mac bought in any year. The act also created a new financial regulator for the two corporations in the Office of Federal Housing Enterprise Oversight (OFHEO). The OFHEO was located in the Department of Housing and Urban Development and, unlike the other federal agencies that regulated financial corporations, it was funded by Congress on an annual basis.[42] Under the legal framework established for OFHEO's regulations, Fannie Mae and Freddie Mac could operate with a minimum capital requirement in relation to assets of 2.5 per cent, a figure much lower than those to which other regulated financial corporations were subject.

In 1994, Fannie Mae pledged $1 trillion in mortgage purchases for ten million low- and moderate-income families to meet these new targets for various low-income groups. However, the Clinton administration wanted the two mortgage corporations to make a more radical shift in approach than those under which they were obliged by the commitments it inherited. In December 1995, the Department of Housing and Urban Development, under Clinton's appointee Henry Cisneros, increased Fannie Mae and Freddie Mac's target for low and moderate-income groups to 42 per cent of total purchases and for special affordable housing to 12 per cent.[43] From 1995 the administration also allowed Fannie Mae and Freddie Mac to buy sub-prime mortgage-backed securities to meet their targets.[44] From 1997, the first sub-prime lending boom faded after default rates rose and a significant number of sub-prime lenders filed for bankruptcy. The Clinton administration responded by increasing its pressure on the two mortgage corporations to support the sub-prime market so that interest rates would fall and liquidity in the mortgage-backed securities market would increase.[45] As a result, in 1998, Fannie Mae introduced a new mortgage product for low-income borrowers, and in October 2000, it announced that it would buy $2 billion of mortgage-backed securities guaranteed by CRA loans. In November 2000, Clinton's second Housing and Urban Development Secretary, Andrew Cuomo, increased the targets that Fannie Mae and Freddie Mac had to meet to 50 per cent for low- and moderate-income earners, to 20 per cent from 14 per cent for the special affordable housing category, and to 31 per cent from 24 per cent for cities, rural areas and underserved communities.[46] This meant that nationally 70 per cent of the two corporations' purchases had to be mortgages for low-income citizens or be securities backed by them.

In its second term the Clinton administration also decided to push Fannie Mae and Freddie Mac to engage in a more proactive way with the issues about minorities embedded in low-income and sub-prime lending. In 1999 the Department of Housing and Urban Development investigated allegations that the automated underwriting systems used by Fannie Mae and Freddie Mac to determine whether applicants were creditworthy facilitated discrimination against minority households. The investigation forced Fannie Mae and Freddie Mac to change their software. The comments of Fannie Mae's chief executive officer, Franklin Raines, in explaining the decision graphically demonstrated how committed Fannie Mae was becoming to lending to the income groups prioritised by the administration:

> There are ... people out there who are so financially distressed that simply getting a 'yes' is the most important thing for them, and the faster you can get to 'yes', the more quickly you've given them the major aspect of the product that they want.[47]

In 1999, Fannie Mae announced that it would formally ease the credit requirements on loans that it would purchase and would do so in part to increase loans to low-income minority groups.[48] That year it also changed its mission statement to emphasise its new commitment to minorities:

> Our mission is to tear down barriers, lower costs and increase the opportunities for home ownership and affordable rental housing for all Americans. Because having a safe place to call home strengthens families, communities and our nation as a whole.[49]

Nonetheless, the pressure from the Clinton administration continued. In March 2000 William Apgar, the federal housing commissioner in the Department of Housing and Urban Development, said that Fannie Mae and Freddie Mac were not doing enough to buy loans made to African-American borrowers and as a result borrowing costs were higher for this group of Americans than whites.[50] Whether *de facto* discrimination continued, Fannie Mae had by 2000 become a significant player in sub-prime lending, particularly African-Americans and Hispanics. It had created new low-income mortgage products targeted at these groups, it had an African-American chief executive officer in Franklin Raines, and it had cultivated a new public rhetoric about the inclusiveness of the American dream of home ownership. Between 1993 and 2001, Fannie Mae's lending to African-Americans increased over 190 per cent, and to low-income families by over 210 per cent.[51]

The Clinton administration's policies on home ownership achieved their aim. Between 1992 and 2000, home ownership increased from 64.1 per cent to 67.7, leaving the rate above that the administration committed itself in 1994 to achieving. In absolute terms, this meant that there were nine million more owner-occupied households at the end of the Clinton presidency than at the beginning.[52] A significant part of this increase came about because lenders made more mortgages to low-income earners than during the previous 50 years of a federally-supported mortgage market. Between 1993 and 2000 the number of mortgage loans to low-income households grew by 70 per cent.[53] The expansion of home ownership was also the product of more lending to African-Americans and Hispanics. From 1994 to 2000, home ownership among whites rose from 70 to 73.8 per cent, among African-Americans from 42.3 to 47.2 per cent and for Hispanics from 41.2 to 46.3 per cent, proportionate increases of 5.4, 11.5 and 12.3 per cent respectively. This expansion of mortgage finance to minorities was supported by the federal home ownership agencies; in 1999 around 37 per cent of loans insured by the FHA went to minority households compared to only 15 per cent of non-FHA loans.[54]

The Clinton administration's policies towards home ownership were not seriously ideologically contested and did not become part of the intense partisan battle between Democrats and the Republicans that characterised much of the Clinton years. There was only modest resistance from congressional Republicans to the administration's approach towards Fannie Mae and Freddie Mac, and most Republicans actively supported those legislatives moves in the last years of the Clinton administration that encouraged more mortgage securitisation and the phenomenal rise in mortgage-backed securities. Sub-prime lending sat just as readily with free-market minded Republicans' political purposes as those of Democrats concerned about income inequality and its social consequences. Asked about sub-prime lending after the market had crashed, the former Republican Senator, Phil Gramm, who had sponsored the Financial Services Modernisation Act, replied:

> Some people look at subprime lending and see evil. I look at subprime lending and I see the American dream in action. My mother lived it as a result of a finance company making a mortgage loan that a bank would not make.[55]

Whilst some Democrats and Republicans did sometimes have different conceptions about how interventionists the American state should be in advancing home ownership through sub-prime lending, the parties generally did not disagree about the end itself.

Through the various moves made by the Clinton administration there was a striking degree of interest group activity. Whilst the issue of home ownership had long generated fierce lobbying groups, particularly from the construction sector, new non-producer advocacy groups became more significant in the 1990s, particularly in the wake of the amendments to the Community Reinvestment Act, and they coalesced around low-income lending. They organised to lobby in Washington and helped create a coalition in Congress that was acutely sensitive to any perceived threat to the minority home ownership agenda. They also pressured individual banks into more lending, particularly to minorities, and to stop predatory loans through legal action and direct action. Primary mortgage lenders responded by setting up community development corporations and co-opting the rhetoric of inclusive home ownership that the Clinton administration had cultivated and the advocacy groups deployed. By the turn of the century, politicians across both parties, an array of advocacy groups and a range of financial corporations, including Fannie Mae and Freddie Mac, were all for different reasons wed to the idea of extending mortgages to more low-income households. Although the expression of that end in sub-prime lending came out of innovations in the financial markets, the rise of these kind of mortgages and the securitisation on which they depended, was also a political phenomenon, and one which had grown out of the vexed political history of state intervention in home ownership in the United States.

## Conclusions

The United States has had a very interventionist state in the financing of home ownership because for more than 70 years the American federal government has not wanted the mortgage outcomes that the market would have produced by itself. Left to their own devices, financial corporations would have made fewer mortgage loans at a higher rate of interest and the number of home owners in the United States would have been smaller, and the power of the American state has been deployed to avert such an outcome. The Hoover and Roosevelt administrations created a *de facto* system of state-insured investment for mortgage lenders during a deep economic crisis and their successors maintained much of it and expanded it through more prosperous times. When there was a risk of another collapse of the mortgage market in the 1980s, the politicians in power in Washington used the fiscal resources of the American state to prevent that possibility as decisively as their predecessors had in the 1930s. Whilst this system did not extend automatically to the new sub-prime lenders of the 1990s the growing involvement of Fannie Mae and Freddie Mac in the sub-prime market eventually took the federal government into this area too. As the federal government played a large role in determining the kind of loans Fannie Mae and Freddie Mac should purchase, and implicitly sustained their opportunity to borrow cheaply to expand rapidly in the market for sub-prime mortgage-backed securities, the American state was, by the end of the 1990s, enmeshed in that part of the mortgage sector too. Although the federal government was never likely to bailout specialist sub-prime lenders, neither was it conceivable that any President could let Fannie Mae or Freddie Mac collapse under the wake of sub-prime liabilities or the debt acquired to make sub-prime purchases, whatever the formality of the charters stating that the two corporations were financially on their own where any such liabilities were concerned.

As the Clinton administration moved to involve the federal government in the sub-prime market, the legacy of racial discrimination and segregation that the federal home ownership agencies had sustained and encouraged between the 1930s and the 1960s was a difficult burden. Politically the past had to be redressed and Fannie Mae and Freddie Mac as government-aided corporations had to be seen to be part of the attempted solution to the very lob-sided social composition of home ownership that had prevailed for so long. However, the political move made by Clinton towards offering tacit federal support to at least some sub-prime lending to minorities merged two questions that economically were far from the same thing with what would become acutely problematic consequences. Ensuring that households from minority groups who were as creditworthy as their white counterparts got equal access to credit was a different issue from whether it was wise to introduce some form of the American state's guarantee on mortgage lending into a market that was extending the pool of those who on the basis of their income, employment and assets were deemed creditworthy. Fusing the two together meant that any political objection to the second approach was rather easily turned into an attack on the equality principle enshrined in the first aim. Whilst it had its practical advantages in sustaining political support for sub-prime lending generally and helped to ensure that more loans were made, it would also have several deleterious consequences. It worked over the next decade to shut down discussion of the political and economic risks inherent to sub-prime lending. Eventually it pushed those who wanted to insist that the leverage that made large-scale sub-prime lending possible was not financially prudent into potentially direct opposition to the whole set of political terms on which Fannie Mae and Freddie Mac operated. During the Bush jnr years the nature of the engagement of the American state in the mortgage market would become politically contested on a more partisan basis than ever before. Yet the very extent of the American state's involvement in financing home ownership in a world in which housing finance had become integrated into international capital markets ensured that there could be no retreat from the state's support for the two mortgage corporations without precipitating an economic disaster.

# 4
# Fannie Mae and Freddie Mac and the Mortgage Boom

The American mortgage boom produced a rise in real house prices of 85 per cent between 1997 and the first half of 2006.[1] This constituted a boom around three times the size of any that had hitherto occurred in the housing market in the United States and perhaps the largest bubble of any asset in history.[2] This new found housing wealth sustained not only large-scale new lending but also a huge re-mortgaging market as households used the equity in their houses to borrow more. This phenomenon drove a significant proportion of consumption after the recession that afflicted the American economy in 2001. Merrill Lynch estimated that around 50 per cent of American growth in the first half of 2005 came directly out of, or was dependent on, the housing sector, and that more than half of the private sector jobs created since 2001 were in housing or housing-related areas.[3] Between 2003 and 2005, the growth residential investment was probably the strongest single force in the American economy, running, as Table 4.1 shows, as it did several times higher than overall growth.[4]

*Table 4.1* Annual real growth as a percentage of GDP, private domestic fixed investment, and residential investment, 2003–2005

| | GDP Growth | Growth in private domestic fixed investment | Growth in residential investment |
|---|---|---|---|
| 2003 | 2.5 | 3.2 | 8.2 |
| 2004 | 3.6 | 7.3 | 9.8 |
| 2005 | 3.1 | 6.5 | 6.2 |

*Source*: United States Bureau of Economic Analysis, National Economic Accounts.

Sub-prime lending of one kind or another was a central part of the mortgage boom. Technically, lending to new groups of borrowers who would hitherto have been deemed un-creditworthy was subdivided into types, sub-prime itself and Alt-A lending. Whilst Alt-A loans were marked as less risky than sub-prime, most Alt-A loans did not require full documentation to show income or assets or employment and some did not require any. Between 2001 and 2005 sub-prime mortgages grew from 7 to 20 per cent of the market and Alt-A mortgages from 2.5 to 12 per cent.[5] Just as significantly, sub-prime and Alt-A lending also drove a boom in mortgage-backed securities. In 2000, financial corporations issued $684 billion of mortgage-backed securities. In 2005 they issued $2.1 trillion.[6] Whilst in 2001 sub-prime and Alt-A constituted 9 per cent of newly originated securitised mortgages, by 2006 they amounted to 40 per cent.[7]

In general, the vast expansion of mortgage-backed securities produced a fundamental problem that in many ways was the central financial cause of the financial crisis: those primary lenders who made the loans to home owners had no continuing interest in whether the borrower could repay. Consequently, these lenders had a strong incentive to take an optimistic view of risk and indeed minimise the standards set for a potential customer to qualify for a loan. By definition, mortgage-backed securities that contained sub-prime and Alt-A loans structurally exposed that problem. Lenders had packed up and sold loans where the risk of default was inherently higher than normal and they had done so having had little motivation to think about acting otherwise in relation to that risk.

For the buyers of securities based on these loans, rationally ignoring this problem depended on there being something else to militate against the risk with which they were encumbering themselves. In practice these buyers appeared to take several steps to negate fear of the risk. First, they assumed that permanently rising house prices effectively eliminated the risk of significant defaults: a borrower who struggled with repayments could sell or re-mortgage on the basis of the rise of equity in the house and, therefore, his or her actual income or assets were irrelevant. Their confidence on this issue received implicit confirmation from the three major rating agencies – Standard and Poor's, Moody's, and Fitch – which gave triple A (investment grade) ratings to mortgage-backed securities that contained sub-prime and Alt-A loans. In retrospect, it is not clear that there was any objective financial basis at all to the judgement that the rating agencies made on sub-prime and Alt-A backed securities. When the sub-prime market began to unravel, Ray McDaniel, the CEO of Moody's told senior managers at the agency:

> [W]hat happened was, it was a slippery slope. ... What happened in '04 and '05 with respect to subordinated tranches is that our competition, Fitch and S&P, went nuts. Everything was investment grade. It didn't really matter. ...
>
> This stuff isn't investment grade. No one cared because the machine just kept going.[8]

A manager at Standard and Poor's said around the same time of the credit rating agencies' denial: 'It could be structured by cows and we would rate it.'[9]

Second, investors in sub-prime and Alt-A mortgage backed-securities purchased credit default swaps as insurance against the possibility of default. Credit default swaps provide a pay-off in the event of a bond or loan the purchaser holds defaulting in return for a premium. These swaps, however, reinforced the problem with these securities rather than solved it. They could be bought in large volume because they were cheap, but that price simply reflected the problematic assumption that there was nothing particularly risky about them in the first place. Indeed, although credit default swaps were designed to reduce the risk of particular portfolios, they created in this case a systemic risk because of the sheer volume of the swaps that were accumulated, the consequent scale of the exposure of those who issued them, and the denial of the actual risk of sub-prime and Alt-A loans on which their price depended. In reality, if a significant number of sub-prime and Alt-A loans were to go into default, then, as eventually transpired, the liabilities around the financial sector would be enormous.

By 2005, sub-prime and Alt-A mortgage-backed securities had become an integral part of the whole American financial sector.[10] As well as holding large portfolios of these securities, the Wall Street investment banks were also issuing mortgage-backed securities themselves, purchasing loans directly from the original lenders rather than buying securities issued by Fannie Mae and Freddie Mac. In becoming large players in this market, the investment banks substantially increased their borrowing, intensifying the risks that their involvement with sub-prime and Alt-A securities created. For example, between 2003 and 2007 Merrill Lynch increased its short-term debt from $111.7 billion to $316.5 billion and its long-term debt from $85.2 billion to $261 billion.[11] This increased debt arose in part because negative real interest rates between October 2002 and November 2005 created an incentive for all corporations to borrow. But, more crucially, the investment banks created a particular opportunity for themselves to increase their leverage rapidly. In 2004, they persuaded the Securities and Exchange Commission to exempt their brokerage units from a net capital regulation, dating back to 1996, which restricted the amount of debt that they could hold. Freed up to borrow more, the investment banks then masked many of the mortgage-backed securities they held by removing them from their balance sheets and placing them in what were termed Structured Investment Vehicles. These were funds set up so that banks could borrow short-term money at low rates of interest and use that money to buy long-term securities and bonds at higher rates of interest. In effect, they allowed banks to increase their borrowing without breaching minimum capital requirements.

Fannie Mae and Freddie Mac were large players in the general mortgage boom. By 2003 the two corporations held or guaranteed 43 per cent of the mortgage market.[12] There were three aspects to their activities: the loans they purchased from primary lenders, the mortgage-backed securities they issued on the basis of these loans, and the mortgage-backed securities investment portfolios they held. Until 2004, Fannie Mae and Freddie Mac were significantly involved in the sub-prime and Alt-A markets through the third activity but not the first two. The 1992 Federal Housing Enterprises Financial Safety and Soundness Act had given the Office of Federal Housing Enterprise Oversight (OFHEO) no regulatory authority over the two mortgage corporations' investment portfolios and since then each had built up large mortgage-backed securities portfolios and in Fannie Mae's case a massive one. Between 1990 and 2003 Fannie Mae's total portfolio rose from $288 billion to $1.3 trillion and Freddie Mac's from $316 billion to $769 billion.[13] They bought 44 per cent of the market.[14] In 2004 Fannie Mae and Freddie Mac each changed business strategy on the first two of their activities, and began to purchase far more sub-prime and Alt-A loans and

*Table 4.2* Sub-prime and Alt-A lending in billions of 2007 dollars, 2003–2005

| | Sub-prime | Alt-A |
|---|---|---|
| 2003 | 349 | 96 |
| 2004 | 593 | 209 |
| 2005 | 663 | 403 |

*Source*: Joint Centre for Housing Studies of Harvard, 'The state of the nation's housing 2008', Harvard University, p. 39.

packaged them into the mortgage-backed securities they issued. Their move produced a significant rise in sub-prime and Alt-A loans, as sub-prime primary lenders had two new large customers in the secondary market.

Once Fannie Mae and Freddie Mac purchased sub-prime and Alt-A loans in significant quantity, they consequently issued more sub-prime and Alt-A backed securities too.

## The Bush administration and the political battle over Fannie Mae and Freddie Mac 2003–5

The housing boom served the Bush jnr's administration's policy aspirations on home ownership. For all the general differences in domestic approach between the Clinton and Bush administrations, on home ownership there was considerable continuity. Just like Clinton, Bush wanted to expand home ownership, particularly for African-Americans and Hispanics. As Lawrence Lindsey, Bush's first chief economic advisor later said: 'No one wanted to stop that bubble. It would have conflicted with the president's own policies.'[15] In June 2002, the administration announced a plan to increase the number of minority home owners by at least 5.5 million by 2010 and said that it wanted the mortgage sector to generate $1 trillion worth of new lending to make that possible. More specifically, it proposed an American Dream Downpayment Fund to give financial aid for down-payments to 40,000 households a year; an affordable housing tax credit for the production of 200,000 homes that low-income families could purchase; a private/public partnership scheme called 'Blueprint for the American Dream'; and increased federal money for community-based self-help ownership programmes.[16] In late 2003, Congress passed, and President

Bush signed into law, the American Dream Downpayment Act, which established a federal fund worth $200 million to be administered by the Department of Housing and Urban Development. This legislation made Federal Housing Agency-insured loans available to those who did not have a down payment. The bill passed unanimously in the Senate and without objection in the House.[17] In response to Bush's initiative, Fannie Mae and Freddie Mac began several new joint lending programmes with primary mortgage lenders, faith-based community groups, and housing advocacy organisations under names such as 'Catch the Dream' and the 'Walk to Worship Mortgage'. Fannie Mae and Freddie Mac were a crucial part of Bush's minority home ownership agenda. They had the practical capacity to deliver more lending and the public rhetoric that they had politically used to justify their unique status equated home ownership, the American dream and minority rights and sat easily with the administration's own language in this policy area.

However, during 2003 the alliance between the Bush administration and Fannie Mae and Freddie Mac was damaged and, as it was, the operations of the two mortgage corporations became sharply politically contested. In some ways the fracturing of the political consensus around Fannie Mae and Freddie Mac had its roots in the late 1990s when the growing size of their mortgage-backed securities portfolios and the borrowing done to procure them began to worry the Clinton administration. In autumn 1999, the then Treasury Secretary, Lawrence Summers, had declared that 'debates about systemic risk should also now include government-sponsored enterprises (GSEs), which are large and growing rapidly'.[18] The following year, the Clinton administration supported an unsuccessful bill that would have ended the Treasury's authority to buy $2.25 billion of each corporation's debt and thus remove one of the protections that allowed them both to take large risks. By 2004, even Alan Greenspan, who generally appeared in public as optimistic as any one about the way that the financial markets were functioning during the mortgage and financial boom, expressed serious concerns about the risks the two corporations were running, telling the Senate Banking Committee that they were under-capitalised, over-leveraged, and that their capacity to issue debt should be restricted:

> The Federal Reserve is concerned about the growth and the scale of the government-sponsored enterprises' mortgage portfolios. ...

> Unlike many well-capitalized savings and loans and commercial banks, Fannie and Freddie have chosen not to manage that risk by holding greater capital. ... Without the expectation of government support in a crisis, such leverage would not be possible without a significantly higher cost of debt.[19]

This growing sense in the Treasury and the Federal Reserve that there were potentially serious safety and soundness issues at Fannie Mae and Freddie Mac turned into something more politically significant with the revelations during 2003 and 2004 that the two corporations were engaged in serious accounting malpractices not dissimilar to the kind that had produced the downfall of Enron and the criminal prosecution of its senior officers. The public exposure of this problem began when OFHEO put Freddie Mac under scrutiny after a change in the corporation's auditors in 2002 revealed that its financial reporting was problematic. In January 2003, Freddie Mac announced that it would have to restate its financial reports for the previous three years. Six months later, OFHEO announced that it would be making a special examination of the company's accounting, which prompted the departure of Freddie Mac's three top executive officers. In November 2003, OFHEO released a report on that examination, which showed how the company had manipulated its reported earnings. In passing judgement, OFHEO declared that the corporation had weak accounting, auditing and internal controls and had shown a disdain for disclosure standards.[20] Eventually Freddie Mac had to restate earnings by $6.9 billion.[21] Prompted by what this inquiry had revealed, OFHEO turned its attention to Fannie Mae. In September 2004, it released an interim report on an ongoing investigation and accused Fannie Mae's executive officers of engaging deliberately and systematically in accounting malpractices in order to achieve earnings goals and receive higher compensation. Consequently, OFHEO declared that it had serious 'concerns regarding the validity of previously reported financial results, the adequacy of regulatory capital, the quality of management supervision, and the overall safety and soundness of the Enterprise'.[22] OFHEO then imposed an agreement on Fannie Mae that required it to set up an external accounting review and reform its organisational and staff structure, its executive compensation operations, its governance and internal controls. OFHEO also demanded that Fannie Mae maintain an additional 30 per cent of capital above the minimum requirement because of the risks it had run.

Fannie Mae responded vociferously to the report and accused OFHEO of launching an ideological attack on its entire existence. Effectively refusing to accept the report, its chief executive officer, Franklin Raines, petitioned the Securities and Exchange Commission to review OFHEO's understanding of Generally Accepted Accounting Principles as they related to specific issues raised in the report in the apparent hope that the Commission would nullify the terms of the agreement that OFHEO had levied. But, in December 2004, the Commission ruled that Fannie Mae's accounts were indeed not compliant with Generally Accepted Accounting Principles and advised the corporation to restate its financial statements for the four years from 2001. Immediately after the verdict, Franklin Raines and the corporation's chief finance officer resigned.[23]

Even after this decision, Fannie Mae continued to challenge the regulator's legal authority to scrutinise its accounts, and on one occasion one of the corporation's lawyers recommended suing OFHEO. It also engaged in systematic lobbying in Congress to try to curtail the investigation, directing the lobbyists it employed to get members of Congress to request that the Department of Housing and Urban Development launch an enquiry into OFHEO's conduct of the examination and to put clauses in an appropriations bill to reduce the regulator's budget until the director was replaced.[24] The final OFHEO report on its special examination, published in 2006, pronounced that between 1998 and 2004 Fannie Mae had overstated reported income and capital by more than $10 billion to hit earnings targets and their actions 'violated numerous statutory, regulatory, and other standards, constituted unsafe and unsound practices, and created unsafe and unsound conditions'.[25] In May 2006, the corporation agreed a settlement with OFHEO and the Securities Exchange Commission that exacted a $400 million fine, placed limits on its growth and imposed remedial action on internal controls, corporate governance, risk management and accounting.[26]

The accounting revelations about Fannie Mae, in particular, exposed the political fault-line hovering over the expansion of home ownership since the simultaneous growth of sub-prime lending and the push by the Clinton and Bush administrations for Fannie Mae and Freddie Mac to structure their actions so that more low-income households could secure a mortgage. When, in 2004, OFHEO published its interim report on Fannie Mae, Democrats in the House of Representatives lined up to defend the corporation. Their arguments in doing so amounted to little more than the unstated premise that bad things could not be happening at Fannie Mae because by definition that would be a bad thing for home ownership and the housing market, and the country could not politically and economically afford deleterious outcomes in these areas. For these Democrats any discussion at all of the accounting practices of Fannie Mae and Freddie Mac was a threat to the political commitment to expanding home ownership and minority home ownership in particular.

When, in September 2003, OFHEO first announced that it would be investigating Fannie Mae, one Democratic representative in the House, declared at a House Financial Services committee hearing about the impending inquiry:

> I am just pissed off at OFHEO because if it wasn't for you I don't think that we would be here in the first place.[27]

A year later, in an exchange at a hearing of a sub-committee of the same committee after the publication of OFHEO's preliminary report on the matter, the Democrat representative Artur Davis tried to make the future of the housing market the responsibility of the Director of OFHEO, Armando Falcon, for, he charged, mistakenly thinking that Fannie Mae and Freddie Mac's alleged malpractices required public attention:

> Mr Davis: Is it possible that by casting all of these dispersions [sic] and all of these doubts upon the board at Fannie Mae, and upon the structure of Fannie Mae, that you potentially are weakening this institution in the market, that you are potentially weakening the housing market in this country?
>
> Are those possible consequences from the very broad and sweeping generalizations you have made about this institution? .... Is that possible? ...
>
> Mr Falcon: If we did our job [im]properly perhaps, but we have not. Congressman, let me just say, I understand your politics running all the issues. ... We are just trying to do our job as a regulator. You can question my motives, my judgment, even my qualifications.

> Mr David: That is not the question I am asking. ... Is it possible that the market standing of Fannie Mae could be weakened by your testimony?
>
> Mr Falcon: It is possible. And if does [sic]
>
> Mr Davis: Thank you, you have answered my question.
>
> Mr Falcon: Course of actions we have taken, it is because of what the company has done, as we have outlined in this report.[28]

Another Democratic representative, Lacy Clay went further and turned defending Fannie Mae's accounting practices into a matter of racial equality, the issue from which, given American's housing history, expanding home ownership could never be separated:

> This hearing is about the political lynching of Franklin Raines. We have seen this happen too many times before. We are to go out of session and the deed is to be done before the election. Why can't we just say that this is the agenda?[29]

By contrast, some Republicans on the House Financial Services Committee were not willing to accept these political terms of debate, and in defending OFHEO tried to establish the narrative of discussion around the financial risk that the Treasury and the Federal Reserve Board believed the two mortgage corporations were running. At the same committee hearing in October 2004, a Republican member, Christopher Shays, moved to defend OFHEO and make the Democrats' denial of the problem the issue:

> I would just like to say to you, Mr. Falcon, what you have done is you have exposed illegal activity on the part of Fannie Mae, and you are being criticized for exposing it. If they have a safety and soundness problem, or if the markets are impacted, it will only be impacted based on what Fannie Mae did. And I just want to congratulate you. You have more courage than I realized you had, because the messenger is being shot and not the person who did the wrongdoing.

> I have seen it here in this committee, and I am pretty outraged by what I am seeing.[30]

Henceforth, the political debate about Fannie Mae and Freddie Mac would unfold within the terms of combat that emerged at these House committee hearings in 2003 and 2004. There was no agreement about what should be at issue in forming policy towards the two corporations, and each side was willing to charge the other with bad faith for insisting on their own narrative as to what was. The future of Fannie Mae and Freddie Mac was now a contested part of American domestic politics and the kind of political divisions that were exposed by the accounting crisis went far beyond practical disagreements about what were the best means to use the two corporations to advance home ownership.

For its part, the Bush administration wanted to engage with the question of financial risk. In September 2003, Bush's then Treasury Secretary, John Snow, unveiled a set of proposals for reforming the regulation of the two corporations. The administration wanted, he said, to replace OFHEO with a financial regulator with more authority. Under the Snow plan, the new regulatory authority would be established within the Treasury and not the Department of Housing and Urban Development. That department, meanwhile, would remain responsible for setting Fannie Mae and Freddie Mac's housing targets and would have its enforcement authority strengthened. The Snow plan also proposed to end the President's authority to nominate five members of the board of each corporation. Testifying on the proposals to the House Financial Services Committee, Snow declared:

> Housing finance is so important to our national economy that we need a strong, world-class regulatory agency to oversee the prudential operations of the government-sponsored enterprises and the safety and soundness of their financial activities consistent with maintaining healthy national markets for housing finance.[31]

Although the specifics differed, the administration's proposals dovetailed with three reform bills initiated by members of Congress that summer which aimed to create a new regulatory structure for the two corporations. In July 2003, a Republican representative from California, Edward Royce, introduced HR 2803, the Housing Finance

Regulatory Restructuring Act of 2003, which would have created a new Office of Housing Finance Oversight Office in the Treasury.[32] The same month, Chuck Hagel, the Republican Senator from Nebraska, introduced S 1508, which would have created an independent regulatory agency, the Federal Housing Enterprise Supervisory Agency. This bill was co-sponsored by Hagel's fellow Republican Senators, Elizabeth Dole, Trent Lott, John McCain, and John Sununu. Two months later, Senator John Corzine, a Democrat from New Jersey, introduced his own bill with provisions for a new regulator.

Although one of these congressional bills was written by a Democrat, the debate about these legislative proposals largely developed along partisan lines, especially in the Senate. In April 2004, the Senate Banking Committee passed S 1508. All the Republicans on the committee voted for passage, and all but one Democrat on the committee, Senator Zell Miller from Georgia, voted against.[33] However, the bill's Republican supporters were unable to get any further action taken on it before the 108th Congress ended. At the beginning of the new Congress, in January 2005, Senators Hagel, Dole and Sununu introduced a new reform bill, S 190. This bill proposed an even tougher regulatory regime than the earlier bills. It would have given the new regulator the right to close down Fannie Mae or Freddie Mac, wider authority over capital requirements and new programmes and activities, and, crucially, limited as a matter of law Fannie Mae and Freddie Mac's investment portfolios of mortgage-backed securities. In July 2005, the Senate Banking Committee once again passed the bill out of committee on a partisan basis.[34] However, the Republican reformers were once again thwarted. Although the Republicans held control of the Senate, without a filibuster-proof majority, they could not get S 190 onto the Senate floor in the absence of support from at least some Democrats, and none was forthcoming. Meanwhile, Fannie Mae and Freddie Mac began a systematic lobbying campaign to break Republican support for the bill. Internal Freddie Mac documents released in 2008 that the corporation targeted 17 Republican Senators to persuade to oppose passage of the legislation.[35] In a last effort to secure a vote on the floor of the Senate, the bill's supporters tried to exploit OFHEO's final damning special examination report, which was published in May 2006. In the hope of using his bipartisan reputation to attract some Democrat support, John

McCain became a co-sponsor of the bill and citing the report declared:

> If Congress does not act, American taxpayers will continue to be exposed to the enormous risk that Fannie Mae and Freddie Mac pose to the housing market, the overall financial system, and the economy as a whole.[36]

But, since many Democrats in Congress had concluded that OFHEO was fundamentally hostile to the two mortgage corporations, the report made little impact. The Republican reformers were still unable to procure any Democrat support for S 190 and the bill was never brought to a Senate vote.

Meanwhile in the House of Representatives a less partisan debate took place over a separate bill, the Federal Housing Finance Reform Act of 2005, sponsored by the Republican representative Richard Baker with 19 fellow Republican co-sponsors. This bill would have created a Federal Housing Finance Agency (FHFA) as an independent new financial regulator with statutory authority over minimum capital requirements and programme approval and discretionary authority over the mortgage-backed securities portfolio. In this last respect it differed significantly from S 190. In eschewing legal limits on the expansion of Fannie Mae and Freddie Mac's investments, the bill attracted significant support from Democrats and passed in the House of Representatives 331–90. Two hundred and nine Republicans voted for the bill and 15 against whilst 122 Democrats voted in favour and 74 opposed passage. Amongst those Democrats voting against were Barney Frank, Maxine Waters and Lacy Clay, all of whom had attacked OFHEO after the accounting revelations for focusing attention in regard to the mortgage corporations on financial risk.[37]

Yet whilst HR 1461 had attracted bipartisan support, it did not ultimately provide the basis of a larger legislative compromise. As the bill was coming to a vote, the Bush administration declared its opposition, arguing that unless Congress placed legal limits on Fannie Mae and Freddie Mac's investment portfolios as S 190 proposed, it was ignoring the central financial risk run by the corporations. That position, however, supposed there was an agreement that financial risk should have priority when those terms of argument had not prevailed. Without such an agreement reform was deadlocked. The Bush administration had been unable to get enough Republicans in the House, where a straight majority vote would have sufficed, to support the kind of regulatory structure that it wanted. Meanwhile, the Republicans in the Senate had failed either to maintain party unity over the issue once Fannie Mae and Freddie Mac intensified their lobbying or procure support from Democrat members, and without some Democrat support they could not overcome the procedural problems that exist in bringing any legislative proposals in that chamber into law.

The Bush administration and the Republicans in the Senate failed in their efforts to re-regulate Fannie Mae and Freddie Mac because they were unable to shift the terms of political debate about the two corporations from the expansion of home ownership to financial risk. In part this was because Fannie Mae and Freddie Mac worked ferociously to try to ensure that they could not. Together they constructed a congressional coalition that would insist at every turn that the issue around the two corporations should be the first and not the second. Both corporations spent large sums of money in different forms to achieve this end. The Centre for Responsive Politics, a non-partisan groups that researches campaign finance, has estimated that $19.3 million went in contributions to members in Congress from Fannie Mae and Freddie Mac or their employees between 1990 and 2008 and that the two corporations spent another $200 million on lobbying.[38] Meanwhile Fannie Mae supplemented this expenditure with the activities of the Fannie Mae foundation. Having created it in 1979, the corporation gave it $350 million of Fannie Mae stock and made it responsible for advertising. Between 2000 and 2005, the foundation gave away $500 million to various organisations, including the Congressional Black Caucus whose members proved a bedrock of political support for the two corporations in the battle over regulation.[39] Whilst these kind of activities were the stuff that virtually all large American corporations engage in to try to influence legislation, some of what Freddie Mac practiced was illegal, and in April 2006, the Federal Electoral Commission fined the company $3.8 million, the largest fine it had ever imposed, for violation of campaign contribution laws. Many of these illegal activities, which included using corporate resources to raise funds for members of Congress directly, serviced the members of the House Financial Services Committee during the time when HR 1461 was under discussion, especially the then Republican Chairman, Michael Oxley.[40]

During the legislative battle over their regulation, Fannie Mae and Freddie Mac also stepped up the rhetoric that they had cultivated since the 1990s that their corporate interests, the sacrosanct principle of home ownership, and American national identity were all the same thing, and they encouraged their congressional supporters to do the same thing. As Franklin Raines told the House Financial Services committee in October 2004: 'We like to say we are in the American dream business.'[41] Turning any attempt to tighten regulation into an attack on home ownership *per se* was a tactic that the two corporations had already deployed when the Clinton administration had given its support to removing the authority of the Treasury to buy $2.25 billion of each corporation's debt. After Gary Gensler, an undersecretary at the Treasury, had testified to Congress in support of legislation to achieve this end, a spokesperson for Freddie Mac had declared that 'we think that the statement evidences a contempt for the nation's housing and mortgage markets'.[42] This time, however, Fannie Mae and Freddie Mac went further, embarking upon a public campaign using this rhetorical equation of the corporations' privileges and the national interest to bring direct pressure from voters to bear on members of Congress.

In 2004, whilst the Senate Banking Committee was deliberating on S 1508, Fannie Mae ran a campaign directed at voters, charging that what was at stake were the aspirations of ordinary Americans and the American dream. One television advertisement broadcast in March of that year went:

> Man: Uh-oh
>
> Woman: What?
>
> Man: It looks like Congress is talking about new regulations for Fannie Mae.
>
> Woman: Will that keep us from getting that lower mortgage rate?
>
> Man: Some economists say rates may go up.
>
> Woman: But that could mean we won't be able to afford the new house.
>
> Man: I know.[43]

Meanwhile an automated telephone message campaign told voters: 'Your congressman is trying to make mortgages more expensive. Ask him why he opposes the American dream of home ownership.'[44]

This same language permeated much of the rhetoric of those in Congress opposed either to any regulatory reform or to any move that placed legal limits on the size of Fannie Mae and Freddie Mac's investment portfolios and borrowing. These representatives generally made their case by first denying that there was any issue of financial risk around the two corporations and then saying that for anyone else to suggest that there were was could only be because those persons were opposed to affordable home ownership. For example, at the hearings held by the House Financial Services Committee immediately after the Bush administration had first proposed reform of Fannie Mae and Freddie Mac's regulatory structure, Barney Frank began by insisting that there could be no safety and soundness issues at the corporations unless they were recognised as such by the corporations' chief executive officers:

> Mr Frank: ... Let me ask [George] Gould and [Franklin] Raines on behalf of Freddie Mac and Fannie Mae, do you feel that over the past years you have been substantially under-regulated? Mr. Raines?
>
> Mr Raines*:* No, sir.
>
> Mr Frank*:* Mr. Gould?
>
> Mr Gould*:* No, sir ...
>
> Mr Frank*:* OK. Then I am not entirely sure why we are here. ... Fannie Mae and Freddie Mac do very good work and they are not endangering the fiscal health of this country.[45]

He later concluded that even considering the issue of financial risk got in the way of the real issue for the future, which was expanding home ownership:

> The more people, in my judgment, exaggerate a threat of safety and soundness, the more people conjure up the possibility of serious financial losses to the Treasury, which I do not see. I think we see entities that are fundamentally sound financially and withstand some of the disastrous scenarios. And even if there were a problem, the Federal Government doesn't bail them out.

> But the more pressure there is there, then the less I think we see in terms of affordable housing.[46]

Similarly, the African-American Democratic representative, Maxine Waters, repudiated any idea that Fannie Mae and Freddie Mac were running risks and tried to return the issue to expanding minority home ownership:

> I have sat through nearly a dozen hearings where, frankly, we were trying to fix something that wasn't broke. Housing is the economic engine of our economy, and in no community does this engine need to work more than in mine. ... We do not have a crisis at Freddie Mac, and in particular at Fannie Mae, under the outstanding leadership of Mr. Frank Raines. Everything in the 1992 act has worked just fine.[47]

Sometimes this line of argument was supplemented with a second, which conceded a little more to the claim that the two corpoations carried a financial risk but insisted that expanding home ownership had to trump any other consideration. In the same committee hearing, Barney Frank finished his comments with an impassioned plea to ignore financial risk:

> I do not want Fannie and Freddie to be just another bank. If they were not going to do more than another bank would because they have so many advantages, then we do not need them. And so therefore, I do think I do not want the same kind of focus on safety and soundness that we have in [the] Office of the Comptroller of the Currency and [the] Office of Thrift Supervision. I want to roll the dice a little bit more in this situation towards subsidised housing.[48]

From this perspective, the absence of a tougher regulator and the consequent opportunity for risk-taking was precisely what made the two mortgage corporations economic and political assets.

When it mattered between 2003 and 2005, Fannie Mae and Freddie Mac were able to maintain a sufficiently broad coalition of support in Congress to defeat the efforts by the Bush administration and Republican reformers in the Senate to create a tighter regulatory structure over them, despite the huge blow that the accounting scandals might have been expected to deliver to their financial credibility. The political debate that had ensued occurred between two opposing narratives about what was at stake and had in part been a partisan battle between Republicans and Democrats in which Republicans prioritised financial risks and Democrats put a higher premium on housing. However, the politics of the two mortgage corporations was also more complex than this partisan polarity suggested. There were Democrats in the House who supported some regulatory reform and there were Republicans in the Senate who had retreated from any radical reform once Fannie Mae and Freddie Mac put them under severe lobbying pressure. Moreover, the Bush administration at no stage wanted to abandon its project to procure 5.5 million new African-American and Hispanic home owners by 2010. In November 2004, the Department of Housing and Urban Development announced that it was increasing the target for each corporation for low- and moderate-income earners from 50 to 56 per cent and for underserved areas from 36 to 39 per cent by 2008.[49] Without any new restrictions on the size of their investment portfolios, this created an even stronger incentive for Fannie Mae and Freddie Mac to buy sub-prime securities that could be used to meet those targets. For all the political capital the Bush administration had expended on trying to establish a regulator that could get tough with the two corporations about the financial risks they were running, ultimately it was unwilling to let go of a home ownership agenda that directly and indirectly encouraged at least some of these risks to be taken.

## Fannie Mae and Freddie Mac's move into sub-prime and Alt-A loans

Whilst the political debate about Fannie Mae and Freddie Mac between 2003 and 2006 played out in Washington, the American mortgage market in which the two corporations operated was changing and in ways that were not immediately beneficial to them. The conjunction of the political scrutiny precipitated by the accounting revelations and the entry of the investment banks and other financial corporations into the market for issuing mortgage-backed securities produced a particular corporate problem for Fannie Mae and Freddie Mac. For a long time, the two corporations had been the largest single issuers of mortgage-backed securities. In 2003, with Ginnie Mae, they had issued 76 per cent of such securities. By 2005 that figure was down to 45 per cent.[50] Over these two years Fannie Mae in particular lost a significant amount of business from its biggest client, Countrywide. The senior executives at both corporations were desperate to reverse this market loss but faced a problem in doing so. Since the new issuers of mortgage-backed securities were willing to buy large amounts of sub-prime and Alt-A loans to package up as securities, Fannie Mae and Freddie Mac could not reclaim their competitiveness without purchasing on a large scale the same kinds of loans themselves and they had hitherto largely eschewed them. Faced with this market imperative, the two corporations changed their approach and moved in their lending activities into the sub-prime and Alt-A sectors. Between 2005 and 2008, Fannie Mae purchased or guaranteed around $270 billion of sub-prime and Alt-A loans, a figure three times higher than all their previous acquisitions from this part of the mortgage market.[51] Almost half of the mortgages that Fannie Mae held had sub-prime or Alt-A characteristics. By the first half of 2007 about 40 per cent of Fannie Mae's new business was Alt-A or interest-only mortgages, having been 26 per cent in 2005.[52] The corporation also stepped up during these three years its purchases of sub-prime mortgage-backed securities for its investment portfolio.[53] Freddie Mac moved in the same direction. In 2004, it changed its risk standards policy, which led to a massive increase between 2005 and 2007 in its purchase of sub-prime and Alt-A loans. Some individuals at both corporations were worried that the financial risks of decisively entering the sub-prime and Alt-A loan market were enormous. In 2004, the chief risk officer at Freddie Mac wrote an e-mail to the chief executive officer, Richard Styron, saying that the company should exit the market for purchasing loans with no income or no asset requirements:

> Freddie Mac should withdraw from the NINA (No Income, No Assets) market as soon as practicable. Our presence in this market is inconsistent with a mission-centred company and creates too much reputation risk for the firm.[54]

However, the senior executives at Freddie Mac wanted to reclaim the market share they had lost on whatever terms the market demanded, and fired the chief risk officer.[55] By 2006 Fannie Mae and Freddie Mac were the largest single purchasers of sub-prime and Alt-A loans.[56] In entering that market, the two corporations pushed the sub-prime and Alt-A boom to its 2005 peak and kept it going through 2007 when other lenders had retreated.

## Foreign central banks and Fannie Mae and Freddie Mac's liabilities

The capital that sustained the whole American mortgage boom in significant part came from abroad. Between June 2002 and June 2006, liabilities to foreigners in the mortgage sector rose by more than 1000 per cent, and the vast proportion of that increase was accumulated in one year between June 2004 and June 2005.

*Table 4.3* Foreign holdings of securities in the thrift and mortgage sector in billions of dollars, June 2002–June 2007

| | Holdings |
|---|---|
| June 2002 | 14.3 |
| June 2003 | 18.8 |
| June 2004 | 19 |
| June 2005 | 130 |
| June 2006 | 189 |

*Source*: United States Department of the Treasury, Reports on foreign portfolio holdings of US securities, 2003–2007.

This rise was almost entirely brought about by an increase in debt rather than equity:

*Table 4.4* Foreign holdings of equity and debt in the thrift and mortgage sector in billions of dollars, June 2002–June 2007

| | Equity | Debt |
|---|---|---|
| June 2002 | 3.8 | 11 |
| June 2003 | 5.7 | 13 |
| June 2004 | 10 | 9.6 |
| June 2005 | 13 | 117 |
| June 2006 | 16.3 | 168.2 |

*Source*: United States Department of the Treasury, Reports on foreign portfolio holdings of US securities, 2003–2007.

Fannie Mae and Freddie Mac were typical corporations in the mortgage sector where such liabilities were concerned in several respects. As Table 4.5 shows, between 2000 and 2007 their total liabilities more than doubled.

*Table 4.5* Fannie Mae and Freddie Mac's liabilities in billions of dollars, 2000–2007

| | Fannie Mae debt outstanding | Fannie Mae MBSs outstanding | Freddie Mac debt outstanding | Freddie Mac MBSs outstanding | Total |
|---|---|---|---|---|---|
| 2000 | 642.7 | 706.7 | 426.7 | 706.7 | 2482.8 |
| 2001 | 763.4 | 863.4 | 578.3 | 863.4 | 3068.5 |
| 2002 | 841.3 | 1040.4 | 665.7 | 1040.4 | 3587.8 |
| 2003 | 961.3 | 1300.5 | 739.6 | 1300.5 | 4301.9 |
| 2004 | 953.1 | 1408 | 731.7 | 1408 | 4500.8 |
| 2005 | 764 | 1598.9 | 748.8 | 1598.9 | 4710.6 |
| 2006 | 767 | 1777.6 | 744.3 | 1777.6 | 5066.5 |
| 2007 | 796.3 | 2118.9 | 738.6 | 2118.9 | 5772.7 |

*Source*: OFHEO, 2008, OFHEO report to Congress, pp. 83 and 100.

Moreover, as Table 4.6 shows, much of the new debt that they issued during the decade was bought by foreigners, leaving them significantly more dependent on foreign capital from abroad by 2007 than they were at the beginning of the decade.

*Table 4.6* Percentage of debt issued by the Agencies held by foreigners, 2000–2007

| | Per cent |
|---|---|
| March 2000 | 7.3 |
| June 2002 | 10.2 |
| June 2003 | 11.3 |
| June 2004 | 11.2 |
| June 2005 | 14.1 |
| June 2006 | 17.2 |
| June 2007 | 21.4 |

*Source*: United States Department of the Treasury, Report on foreign portfolio holdings of US Securities, 2007, p. 8.

However, in two respects Fannie Mae and Freddie Mac's borrowing was different than that of other financial corporations. Even by the standards of leverage of the mortgage and financial boom, the two corporations had borrowed from the 1990s on a vast scale. In 2003 Fannie Mae operated with a ratio of total capital to total assets of just over 3 per cent and Freddie Mac of just under 4 per cent compared to a ratio across federally-insured depository corporations of over 9 per cent.[57] They also had access to creditors to whom others did not. As investors believed that their liabilities would in the final instance have to be backed by the American government, foreign central banks looking to purchase dollar assets were willing to buy their bonds and securities. Large-scale lending from foreign central banks to Fannie Mae and Freddie Mac began at the turn of the century. As the local currency loss on accumulating Treasury bonds increased in 2006, Fannie Mae and Freddie Mac's bonds and securities, which delivered some interest premium over the government's issuance, escalated until by 2007 foreign central banks held more than a trillion dollars' worth of the two corporation's long-term bonds and securities, as Table 4.7 illustrates. Whilst the value of foreign holdings of Treasury bonds had been nearly 700 per cent of those of agency bonds in 1994, by June 2007 it was just 150 per cent.

*Table 4.7* Foreign holdings of long-term securities issued by the US Treasury and the Agencies in billions of dollars, 1994–2004

| | **Treasury** | **Agencies** |
|---|---|---|
| December 1994 | 333 | 48 |
| March 2000 | 884 | 261 |
| June 2002 | 908 | 492 |
| June 2003 | 1116 | 586 |
| June 2004 | 1426 | 619 |
| June 2005 | 1599 | 791 |
| June 2006 | 1727 | 984 |
| June 2007 | 1965 | 1304 |

*Source*: United States Department of the Treasury, Report on foreign portfolio holdings of US securities 2007, p. 6.

Much of this lending was done by a few central banks, particularly the Chinese and the Japanese, leaving them with considerable exposure to Fannie Mae and Freddie Mac's financial performance.

*Table 4.8* Official holdings of China, Japan, South Korea, Taiwan and Russia of long-term agency debt in billions of dollars, March 2000–June 2007

| | China | Japan | Russia | South Korea | Taiwan |
|---|---|---|---|---|---|
| March 2000 | 19.6 | 42.6 | 3.5 | 14.6 | 4.7 |
| June 2002 | 58.6 | 88 | 2.9 | 7.6 | 25.3 |
| June 2003 | 91.1 | 102.4 | 2.2 | 24.7 | 34.6 |
| June 2004 | 114.9 | 99.8 | 6.2 | 33.8 | 39 |
| June 2005 | 172 | 139.7 | 12.9 | 42.7 | 41 |
| June 2006 | 253.3 | 184.2 | 38.4 | 42.3 | 52.6 |
| June 2007 | 376.3 | 228.1 | 75.3 | 63 | 54.8 |

*Source*: United States Department of the Treasury, Foreign portfolio holdings of US Securities, historical data.

In addition Russia bought significant quantities of the two corporations' short-term debt:

*Table 4.9* Official Russian holdings of short-term agency debt in billions of dollars, March 2000–June 2007

| | Holdings |
|---|---|
| March 2000 | 3.5 |
| June 2002 | 20.9 |
| June 2003 | 30.9 |
| June 2004 | 38.8 |
| June 2005 | 62 |
| June 2006 | 67.6 |
| June 2007 | 38.5 |

*Source*: United States Department of the Treasury, Foreign portfolio holdings of US securities, historical data.

## Conclusions

The fact of Fannie Mae and Freddie Mac's liabilities to foreign central banks created a big disjuncture between the geo-political implications of the economic path the two corporations were able to take and the domestic American political debate about how they should be regulated, what financial risks they should be allowed to run, and the relationship of those risks to the expansion of home ownership for minorities in particular. Even those who were worried about the scale of the corporations' portfolios of mortgage-backed securities and the borrowing on which they depended professed in public, anyway, that the two corporations' liabilities were not ultimately a burden for the American state. For example, Bush's second Treasury Secretary, John Snow, pronounced in 2004:

> Government-sponsored enterprises are able to borrow at rates that are lower than their other financial competitors, other financial institutions, because they are perceived by many in the marketplace to have a relationship with the government; they are perceived to have a government guarantee. Since Fannie and Freddie trade at very narrow spreads to the very best paper in the world, which is the US Treasury, they have become enormous entities, and they are growing at a very, very rapid rate. The debt levels they are issuing are sizable relative to the economy of the United States. To put it into perspective, the US Government debt held by the public is about $3.6 trillion; the government-sponsored enterprises' now totals about $2.4 trillion and when you are that big you have potential significant impacts on financial markets. ...We don't believe in a 'too big to fail' doctrine, but the reality is that the market treats the paper as if the government is backing it. We strongly resist that notion. You know that there is that perception. And it's not a healthy perception and we need to disabuse people of that perception. Investments in Fannie and Freddie are uninsured investments.[58]

For their part, those who were resisting any reform that would constrain the corporations' expansion and operations needed to state publicly that the two corporations were on their own because that premise separated the risks around Fannie Mae and Freddie Mac from the federal budget deficit. If the two corporations were putting themselves in financial jeopardy, their supporters argued, the responsibility lay with the creditors and the shareholders. As Barney Frank put this claim to the House Financial Services Committee in 2003:

> Some of the critics of Fannie Mae and Freddie Mac say that the problem is that the Federal Government is obligated to bail out people who might lose money in connection with them. I do not believe that we have any such obligation... I am a strong sup-

> porter of the role that Fannie Mae and Freddie Mac play in housing, but nobody who invests in them should come looking to me for a nickel – nor anybody else in the Federal Government. And if investors take some comfort and want to lend them a little money and less [sic] interest rates, because they like this set of affiliations, good, because housing will benefit. But there is no guarantee, there is no explicit guarantee, there is no implicit guarantee, there is no wink-and-nod guarantee. Invest, and you are on your own.[59]

Yet the whole international market for the debt and securities that Fannie Mae and Freddie Mac issued relied on the fact that this kind of rhetoric was denial. The credit-rating agency Standard and Poor's had said that the likelihood of 'extraordinary support' from the American government was the reason why it gave the corporations a triple-A rating despite their exceptional leverage.[60] And even if the American government could in a crisis possibly have washed its hands of Fannie Mae and Freddie Mac's liabilities under a scenario in which the corporations' creditors were mostly private domestic investors, it was unthinkable that it could when so much was owed to other states' central banks, especially to ones that in holding huge amounts of other dollar assets could inflict enormous damage on the entire American economy and international financial order if they so chose.

The political debate about Fannie Mae and Freddie Mac in the United States was constructed almost exclusively in domestic terms about whether to prioritise home ownership or protection against financial risk, and evaded the consequences of the indebtedness of the two corporations to foreign creditors and the east Asian central banks in particular. In this sense, the domestic political debate was aired in unreality and un-tuned to the constraints that economic interdependence had created. The potential consequences of this evasion only deepened as Fannie Mae and Freddie Mac ventured further and further into the sub-prime and Alt-A markets. From 2004, the two corporations, neither of which had produced reliable financial reports for several years, were issuing a vast volume of bonds and securities backed by high-risk loans. The financial markets themselves produced no check on what the corporations could borrow and issue, not least because the credit-rating agencies were gripped in the belief that those securities carried little risk. However, the kinds of economic interdependence and power relations that characterised the international economy as it had developed since the Asian financial crisis created their own reality that American politicians could ultimately not escape. The central banks in Asia and elsewhere were buying the securities of Fannie Mae and Freddie Mac because they assumed that wherever the burden of the risk of the corporations' borrowing turned out to fall, it would not be on them. Since they were not only major creditors to the two corporations but huge holders of dollar assets in a context of significant economic interdependence between the United States and east Asia the rhetorical presumption of the domestic political debate that investors had misjudged American promises was ultimately irrelevant. From the outset of Fannie Mae and Freddie Mac's large-scale borrowing from the east Asian central banks, the American state effectively had to act as the guarantor of the corporations' liabilities, unless an American President was prepared to contemplate international financial catastrophe. Crucially, however, it was left in a position where it would have to do so because of the expectations created by its own long involvement with the two corporations. Whilst the options available for the American state were diminished by economic interdependence, it was the domestic political terms on which the American state was engaged with home ownership which had beget the circumstances in which these constraints had their purchase.

# 5
# The Crisis of 2007–8

The American sub-prime mortgage bust of 2006 was inevitable because the whole structure of sub-prime lending and the securitisation of mortgages on which it depended had denied the central risk that defined it. Historically, all financial markets driven to peaks by blind optimism, or, as Alan Greenspan once put it, irrational exuberance have collapsed. Yet financial bubbles also always burst at specific temporal moments for reasons contingent to the events that are happening at that time. The bursting of this particular bubble in 2006 was triggered by the conjunction of stalling house prices from late 2005 and rising interest rates from the second half of 2004, which culminated in the Federal Reserve Board setting a discount rate of 6.25 per cent in June 2006. The fall in house prices in 2006, however initially modest, was a lethal blow to sub-prime and Alt-A borrowers because they needed rising prices to refinance at any time when they were unable to service their loans. Once prices began to fall, potential new sub-prime borrowers became a credit risk, and lenders denied a restructured loan to those who could not meet their monthly payments and foreclosed on their homes. Meanwhile, the rise in interest rates choked demand for new mortgages and increased the cost of non-fixed rate existing mortgages, the first putting further downward pressure on house prices and the second pushing more sub-prime and Alt-A borrowers towards a final default.

Whilst these specific developments were in significant part the consequence of domestic American macro-economic and housing market dynamics, they also in part arose from the international conditions that had made the boom possible. American interest rates were as low as they were between 2000 and 2004 because the east Asian states had been willing to lend to the United States to fund its budget and current account deficits without expecting an interest return to compensate for the risk of dollar depreciation. Those low interest rates were a crucial component of the mortgage boom. When the Federal Reserve Board then began to increase interest rates in late June 2004 inflation was still within the range of 1–2 per cent in which the Federal Reserve hoped to contain it, despite the speed with which prices were still rising at that point in the housing market. In November 2004, with inflation still within the Federal Reserve's range and a set of employment figures that did not suggest new evidence of inflationary pressure, the American central bank raised rates again. The Federal Reserve's decision came in a week in which the dollar fell to a new low against the euro. Whilst nothing in the Federal Reserve's public comments suggested that it was responding to the deterioration of the dollar's position, neither could it have made that motivation explicit without heaping more pressure on the currency. It is hard to avoid the conclusion that the weakness of the currency was at the very least part of the context in which the Federal Reserve set upon a further tightening of monetary conditions that autumn. Whatever the reality behind the Fed's decision, the rise in interest rates through the second half of 2004 and 2005 led to a period of relative dollar strength in 2005 that was sharply at odds with the weakness of the currency in 2002–3 and 2006–7. In acting as it did, the Federal Reserve reduced the short- to medium-term cost to the east Asian states of maintaining their side of the Pacific economic relationship both by offering a higher rate of return on their dollar assets and by temporarily abating the local currency loss they were accepting on their purchases.

The fall of the American sub-prime market played out through 2006 and in the first half of 2007 metastasised into the far wider financial crisis that began in the summer of 2007. Within the sub-prime sector itself, primary lending and the secondary market both effectively collapsed in 2007. During 2006 the defaults on sub-prime and Alt-A loans, especially sub-prime mortgages carrying an adjustable rate, had far exceeded what the credit rating agencies had calculated as likely. By July 2007, nearly 15 per cent of sub-prime adjustable-rate mortgages, almost all of which originated in 2005 and 2006, were more than 90 days late with payment or in foreclosure, compared to around 5 per cent in mid-2005. Some of those who defaulted had made no payments at all.[1] Between November 2006 and September 2007, more than 80 sub-prime mortgage lenders either stopped lending, shut down, declared bankruptcy, or were sold off. In March 2007, America's largest sub-prime lender, New Century Financial, stopped offering mortgages after the firm's creditors refused to lend any more money, the US Attorney's Office for central California began a criminal investigation of the company, and the New York Stock Exchange delisted it. The following month New Century Financial filed for chapter 11 bankruptcy. Three months later, Countrywide Financial, the largest overall mortgage lender said that its problems within the sub-prime and Alt-A sectors were spreading into the prime market. In 2007, the market for mortgage-backed securities also dried up and various money markets funds that had purchased large quantities of these securities went bankrupt. From June 2007 the credit rating agencies began to downgrade any mortgage-backed securities that were not issued by Fannie Mae, Freddie Mac or Ginnie Mae. During the first half of 2007, the sub-prime crisis also began to hurt the overall housing sector of the economy. Having begun to fall in 2006, house prices fell more sharply through 2007 and investment in housing dropped rapidly. In 2007, residential fixed investment fell by 19 per cent in 2007 whilst the sales of new homes fell by 26 per cent and of existing homes by 13 per cent.[2]

In the summer of 2007, the Bush administration and the Federal Reserve made their first significant moves in response to the sub-prime crisis. In August, the Federal Reserve cut interest rates for the first time in more than four years. By the summer of 2008 it had lowered the discount rate to 2.25 per cent. Meanwhile, just as its predecessors had done when home ownership came under pressure, the Bush administration turned to the federal housing agencies and to Fannie Mae and Freddie Mac to support the mortgage market. In August 2007, it announced that the Federal Housing Administration (FHA) would have the authority to insure loans for delinquent borrowers if they had faced interest rate rises. It also pushed Fannie Mae and Freddie Mac to lend more, in particular to those sub-prime borrowers who needed to re-mortgage.[3]

## The sub-prime fallout in the financial sector

The sub-prime crash of 2007 eventually resonated through the whole American financial sector and those of other western states too. It did so primarily because of the nature of the markets in, and around, mortgage-backed securities. Many financial corporations across the world held sub-prime-mortgage backed securities, or collateralised debt obligations – structured asset-backed securities comprising a portfolio of underlying assets offering varying returns – containing them. Other firms had sold credit default swaps on these securities, and obligations, effectively offering insurance against the risk on the original sub-prime loans, a significant number of which were now in default. The first evidence of the broader financial fallout appeared in early 2007. That February, HSBC, Europe's largest bank, wrote down its holdings of mortgage-backed securities by $10.5 billion. Two months later, the large Swiss bank, USB, closed a money fund that had large sub-prime security losses. However, the scale of how much was at stake was not apparent until July 2007. That month, Bear Stearns announced that two of its hedge funds had collapsed because of their losses in mortgage-backed securities. In response, Moody's and Standard and Poor's started downgrading some of these securities and the collateral debt obligations in which they had been placed and announced that they were reviewing others. Accordingly, the markets began to re-price all swaps relating to mortgage-backed securities, which caused the spreads on these derivatives to rise significantly.

Between the third quarter of 2007 and the second quarter of 2008, the credit rating agencies proceeded to lower the ratings of nearly $2 trillion worth of mortgage-backed securities.[4] Once the market price of mortgage-backed securities fell and the cost of insuring them rose, banks and other financial corporations had to face up to the consequences of these developments for their balance sheets. Looking at imminent large losses, they responded by trying to hold on to cash and raise more capital. As a result, in August 2007 in the United States and Europe, all but very short-term inter-bank lending dried up, money-market funds cut off loans, and the price of commercial paper, which makes it possible for corporations to meet short-term debt obligations, rose sharply. Put simply, the American and European financial sectors were on the precipice of a structural crisis. Banks did not trust that other banks were creditworthy because they feared the pervasive general scale of the losses from mortgage-backed securities and credit default swaps that were to come whilst having no clear idea where the particularity of those losses would unfold. To avoid that systemic crisis, the Federal Reserve and other central banks pumped liquidity into the overnight money markets to provide banks with access to short-term credit.

The collapse of confidence and swift contraction of credit markets for the financial sector itself in the summer of 2007 damaged the reputation of American capital markets and raised fundamental questions about the credibility of dollar assets. This was acutely consequential in itself, but it was hugely so in a world in which central banks, and in particular the east Asian central banks, held such large quantities of such assets and which was exposed to all the interdependencies created by the economic relationship between the United States and east Asia. This structural hit to the whole financial sector also hit the mortgage market all over again. Since many sub-prime and some other mortgage lenders relied on capital markets rather than deposits to finance their operations, they now had virtually no access to new funding. Consequently, they were unable to make more loans to try to turn the market around, leaving even more sub-prime borrowers with no option of refinancing and heading towards foreclosure. Meanwhile, the mortgage market appeared unresponsive to the loosening of monetary policy. Indeed, after the Federal Reserve cut the discount rate in September 2007, the mortgage rate on a standard 30-year loan actually rose over the next week.

The scale of the market adjustment around mortgage-backed securities that took place in the summer of 2007 and its consequences for the financial sector as a whole was dramatically reflected in quarterly reports released by the largest financial corporations in the last months of 2007 and early 2008. Merrill Lynch announced an $8.4 billion write-down on its mortgage-related collateralised debt obligation exposure for the third quarter, resulting in a loss of $2.2 billion, at that moment in time the largest ever made by a Wall Street company. Between the beginning of 2005 and the start of 2007, Merrill Lynch had made a significant number of purchases of mortgage lenders, including First Franklin, a specialist sub-prime firm. On the top of the losses that these investments had wrought, the investment bank was exposed because the insurance corporation American International Group (AIG), the largest issuer of credit default swaps in the financial sector, had since late 2005 stopped guaranteeing many of its large portfolio of collateralised debt obligations.[5] With the release of reports for the fourth quarter of 2007, the size of the fallout of the unravelling of mortgage-backed securities descended to another level. Over a matter of weeks in 2008, Merrill Lynch and Citigroup announced losses of $9.8 billion, Morgan Stanley of $3.6 billion, AIG of $5.3 billion, and Bear Stearns of $854 million.[6]

## The sovereign wealth funds: Rescue and withdrawal

Although in the second half of 2007 the world's leading central banks with various measures had been able to maintain the short-term money markets to avoid a financial meltdown, the scale of the losses in the financial sector that accumulated during the third and fourth quarters of that year meant that banks and other financial corporations required new capital to achieve any kind of medium-term recovery. In the prevailing international economy of the first decade of the 21st century, in which savings were distributed as unequally as they were, this meant that, unless the American and European governments were going to bailout their financial corporations with taxpayers' money, the western financial sector had to have access to capital from the rich oil producers or the east Asian states. In late 2007 and early 2008, the sovereign wealth funds of some of those states, including China's, obliged and recapitalised parts of the American financial sector and some European banks too. In doing so, they temporarily saved western governments from a banking crisis, but they also ensured that any future failure of the financial corporations in which they had invested would become a matter of foreign policy for the American government. Between April 2007 and January 2008, the sovereign wealth funds invested around $70 billion in the American financial sector of which $30 billion was offered in December 2007 and January 2008 alone.[7] In December 2007 Morgan Stanley took $5 billion from China's sovereign wealth fund in exchange for a stake of around 10 per cent, and in January 2008 Merrill Lynch took $9.9 billion from the sovereign wealth funds of South Korea, Singapore and Kuwait and Citigroup $14.5 billion from those of Abu Dhabi, Singapore and Kuwait.[8]

Sovereign wealth funds had existed since the 1950s when the Kuwaiti government created the Kuwait Investment Authority to invest the funds of the country's oil revenues. Since the development of an international economy in which net capital flowed into, rather than out, of the western world, other states had followed suit. Between 2000 and 2008, China, South Korea, Taiwan, Russia, Libya, Qatar,

Kazakhstan, the United Arab Emirates and Saudi Arabia all created state investment funds. In light of the complexities of the economic relationship between the United States and east Asia, the most consequential of these was China's. The Chinese government's decision to create such a fund arose in the context of where the inherent burdens of that relationship had left China. Whilst the Chinese leadership was committed to maintaining credit to the United States, the dollar's weakness in 2006 and 2007, and the not insignificant appreciation of the yuan since the autumn of 2006, meant that the price of that relationship was rising for China. During 2007, the yield on long-term Treasury bonds ran between 4.5 per cent and 5 per cent but the yuan appreciated 6 per cent against the dollar, leaving China holding securities at a loss in local currency terms. In March 2007, the Chinese government announced that it would establish a sovereign wealth fund, the China Investment Corporation (CIC), to increase the rate of return on at least some of the state's foreign exchange reserves. In September 2007, the CIC began operating with $200 billion of capital. In the interim, a government agency, the China Jianyin Investment Company, bought a $3 billion stake in the Blackstone Group, an American private equity firm, and the CIC on its inception assumed the investment.

In practice, increasing the rate of return on a proportion of China's foreign exchange reserves meant the CIC finding investments that would yield more than the rate of dollar depreciation took away. However, the nature of this strategic move was transformed by the descent of the American financial sector into crisis in the time between the Chinese government's decision to act in the spring of 2007 and the formation of the CIC six months later. The Chinese leadership had turned to a sovereign wealth fund to try to reduce exchange rate losses, but, once circumstances changed, it found itself confronting the likelihood of a direct loss on the first corporate investment that the CIC held, regardless of what happened to the value of the dollar against the yuan. The size of the losses of the large American financial corporations in the second half of 2007 then created a whole new and intractable dilemma. If China, with other saving-rich states, did not inject capital into the American financial sector, the financial side of the economic relationship between the United States and east Asia would begin to unravel as dollar losses escalated. Yet if China acted to try to save the American financial sector, unless shares for financial corporations recovered reasonably swiftly, it would face new investment losses.

In investing in Merrill Lynch, the CIC responded to the imperative to embark upon a rescue act. But just months later, a crisis at another American investment bank, Bear Stearns, intensified the American financial sector's woes, and it followed the conflicting imperative to withdraw and reverse course. In March 2008, Bear Stearns was heading for insolvency. The previous autumn, a Chinese government-controlled securities firm had reached an agreement with Bear Stearns to buy 6 per cent of the bank in exchange for a return investment. Between late 2007 and March 2008, Bear Stearns' share price fell more than 70 per cent. At the moment of the investment bank's crisis, the Chinese firm said that it would not proceed with the deal. At the same time, the Bank of China said that it was not interested in more investments in western financial firms. With none of the other sovereign wealth funds making capital available either, Bear Stearns had to turn to the Federal Reserve for an emergency loan. When that loan did not stabilise Bear Stearns, the Federal Reserve and the Treasury forced Bear Stearns to sell one of the other American investment banks, JP Morgan. Henceforth, the burden of sustaining the American financial sector would fall on the Federal Reserve and Treasury, or, in other words, the American state.

However, the interdependencies created by the economic relationship between the United States and east Asia ensured that the retreat of the sovereign wealth funds from further involvement in the America financial sector could not easily lead to a more general east Asian withdrawal from dollar assets. The cessation of the money markets and inter-bank lending in August 2007 weakened the dollar and seriously diminished private and official demand for long-term American securities. In August 2007, there was a net sale of $35 billion of these assets by foreigners, and during the last months of 2007 the dollar slid. Demand for long-term securities recovered in the last quarter of 2007 such that there were net monthly purchases for the remaining months of the year and the first six months of 2008, including more than $100 billion in October 2007 alone.[9] However, some foreign investors, including some central banks, had not returned. Henceforth, at moments of particular dollar weakness, the Japanese and Chinese central banks had to step up their purchases. In January 2008, central banks added $52.8 billion to their reserves, more than twice what private investors were willing to buy. As Table 5.1 shows, during the first six months of 2008 central banks ended up buying more than one-third of the long-term securities investors purchased.

*Table 5.1* Private and official net purchases of US-long term securities by foreigners in billions of dollars, January 2007–June 2008

| | **Private** | **Official** | **Total** | **Proportion official** |
|---|---|---|---|---|
| January–June 2007 | 555.5 | 110.3 | 665.8 | 16.6% |
| July–December 2007 | 223.9 | 78.1 | 302 | 25.9% |
| January–June 2008 | 328.8 | 180.5 | 509.3 | 35.4% |

*Source*: United States Department of the Treasury, Monthly reports of cross-border financial flows, January 2007 to June 2008.

The Chinese central bank made these purchases despite the fact that the Federal Reserve cut interest rates three times between December 2007 and January 2008 and the fact that between October 2007 and early January 2008 the yuan rose significantly. Indeed, in not cutting interest rates in response to the Federal Reserve's moves, the Chinese central bank had itself now acquiesced to the upward pressure on the yuan that was magnifying the currency risk of adding to the state's portfolio of dollar assets.

Nonetheless, the east Asian central banks were unable to stop the dollar's slide. For China, this, once again, came at a particular cost. Through the first half of 2008, it was left with the realities that there was no imminent end to the problems in the American financial sector, that the Federal Reserve would make further cuts in interest rate as the risk of the recession increased, and that the exchange rate loss on its dollar investments in various portfolios would mount. What had been private fear about where the financial relationship with the United States had left China, became in 2008 publicly expressed discontent. That April, one official in the Chinese Ministry of Commerce pronounced:

> At a time when the US dollar is in a continuous fall and is thus making a huge mess in the world economy, China should insist on making the US dollar devaluation a topic of the dialogue. The negative results of the US dollar's decline are evident: the rising

> prices of all primary products, the intensified pressure on inflation globally, the confusion in the settlement of international transactions, etc. Worst of all, this is the US's disguised way of avoiding paying off its debts to foreign countries.[10]

Yet whatever the frustrations the Chinese leadership experienced as international circumstances deteriorated for China, the interdependencies created by the economic relationship with the United States still left it limited options in contemplating any alternative strategic approach.

## Fannie Mae and Freddie Mac in crisis

Fannie Mae and Freddie Mac were caught up in every aspect of the crisis that was emerging through the second half of 2007 and early 2008. They had bought up a large number of sub-prime and Alt-A loans; they were huge players in the mortgage-backed securities market, and China held a significant quantity of their liabilities. In 2007, like virtually every company in the mortgage sector, Fannie Mae and Freddie Mac performed poorly. Fannie Mae reported a net loss for the year of $2.1 billion and Freddie Mac of $3.1 billion. Most of each of their losses came from the Alt-A loans that they purchased and securitised. However, for all Fannie Mae and Freddie Mac's financial problems they were also the only means the Bush administration and Congress had from the summer of 2007 to try to resurrect the mortgage market both in primary lending and the issuance and purchase of mortgage-backed securities. That political opportunity existed because investors around the world were still willing to lend Fannie Mae and Freddie Mac in the belief that the American government would stand by their debt, despite the fact that the two firms were even more heavily leveraged than other financial corporations for whom capital markets had become virtually closed, and notwithstanding all the questions that the two corporations' non-reporting left unanswered about the actual states of their balance sheets. As Table 5.2 shows, although the foreign central banks did not purchase the same volume of the long-term securities issued by the two corporations in the year after the sub-prime crisis spread across the financial sector as they had in the first six months of 2007, they were still willing to provide nearly as much credit as they had during 2006.

*Table 5.2* Net official purchases of long-term agency securities in billions of dollars, 2005–2008

| | **Purchases** |
|---|---|
| 2005 | 31.6 |
| 2006 | 92.6 |
| January 2007–June 2007 | 78.9 |
| July 2007–December 2007 | 40.9 |
| January 2008–June 2008 | 47.6 |

*Source*: United States Department of the Treasury, Monthly reports of cross-border financial flows, 2005 to June 2008.

Even during August 2007 when foreign central banks made a net sale of $29.7 billion of Treasury bonds, they made net purchases of $4.1 billion of agency bonds.[11] Whilst few other financial firms were able to buy loans and issue new mortgage-backed securities because they could not borrow new money, Fannie Mae and Freddie Mac increased their issuance of such securities during 2007 by more than 30 per cent. In the fourth quarter of 2007, the two corporations held more than three-quarters of the single-family mortgages originated during the period.[12]

Whilst the Bush administration needed Fannie Mae and Freddie Mac to try to turn the mortgage market around, the regulation of the two corporations remained a politically contested issue. In early 2007, President Bush's Treasury Secretary, Hank Paulson, had reached a compromise with the Democrat chair of the House Financial Services Committee, Barney Frank, on a bill to reform the corporations. In March of that year, Frank introduced HR 1427 with two Democrat and three Republican co-sponsors which the House Financial Services Committee quickly sent to the House floor. HR 1427 would have created a Federal Housing Finance Agency (FHFA) as a new regulator, given that regulatory some discretionary authority over the corporations' investment portfolios, set new capital requirements, and created an affordable housing fund out of Fannie Mae and Freddie Mac's profits, the proceeds of which would be distributed by Congress.[13] On 22 May 2007, the House passed HR 1427 by 313 votes to 104. All the Democrats in the House voted in favour.

This agreement between Frank and Paulson reflected some measure of bipartisan convergence in the terms of debate on Fannie Mae and

Freddie Mac. Frank secured previously sceptical Democrat support for the bill's passage by insisting on the affordable housing clauses of HR 1427. In doing so, he seemed to allow even those on the House Financial Services Committee who had hitherto insisted that regulation was entirely a matter of home ownership to accept that financial risk might be part of the discussion, even if they were not yet ready to acknowledge that there might be any such danger arising from the two corporations' operations at that moment in time. The Democratic Representative, Maxine Waters, who had vociferously defended Fannie Mae through the 2004 hearings on the company's accounting malpractices, commented on the legislation:

> We are all interested in safety and soundness. I know the constant refrain about the fact that these government-sponsored enterprises are too big and that God forbid, they should collapse, but it has been a lot more of the kind of negative questioning and the anticipated problems rather than any real problems within these government-sponsored enterprises as it relates to their soundness.[14]

However, any convergence in the policy discourse only went so far. Immediately HR 1427 passed the agreement between Barney Frank and the Treasury collapsed, as in accepting the legislation, the House adopted on a voice vote a late amendment that minimised the authority of the new regulator over the corporations' investment portfolios, after lobbying from Fannie Mae and Freddie Mac.[15] The Bush administration responded by saying that it wanted a new, tougher bill. Meanwhile the Democrats on the Senate Banking Committee were less keen on even the original HR 1427 than their House counterparts and the bill did not come out of that committee, and the Republican reformers in the Senate still wanted to enact a tougher regulatory bill with statutory limits on the portfolios. In April 2007, the Republican Senators John Sununu, Chuck Hagel, Elizabeth Dole and Mel Martinez introduced the Federal Housing Enterprise Regulatory Reform Act of 2007, S 1100. With the Democrats now in control of the Senate, this reform bill did not get out of the Senate Banking Committee. Once the sub-prime mortgage collapse spread to the financial sector, more disagreement about the corporations ensued, and some Democrats in the House backtracked on their support for new regulatory rules. In October 2007, Barney Frank initiated a bill to suspend some of the requirements that Office of Federal Housing Enterprise Oversight (OFHEO) had imposed on Fannie Mae after the conclusion of the special examination investigation. Although the bill went nowhere, Frank's action suggested that congressional support for any action that significantly constrained the two corporations' activities was now as politically lacking as ever, despite the dramatic demonstration by the middle of 2007 of the inherent dangers of mortgage-backed securities.

With the serious reformers politically defeated, Congress eventually accepted a set of more modest proposals. In July 2007, Democrat representative Nancy Pelosi introduced a new bill, generally similar in content to the amended version of HR 1427 for which the House had finally voted. This bill, HR 3221, passed the House in August 2007 and the Senate in April 2008. The final reconciled bill was passed and signed into law as the Federal Housing Finance Regulation Reform Act in July 2008 as part of the Housing and Economic Recovery Act, which aimed to provide general support to the mortgage sector. The Federal Housing Finance Regulation Reform Act established a Federal Housing Finance Agency (FHFA) as the successor to the OFHEO. It had the authority to establish capital standards and impose some limits on the corporations' expansion, including of their investment portfolios. Like HR 1427, it also created an affordable housing trust fund out of the corporations' profits.

Paradoxically, however, the incentives created by domestic politics continued to protect the two corporations even as a somewhat tougher regulatory regime beckoned. Whilst the Congress was moving to pass this legislation, OFHEO and the Bush administration were also moving to lift some of the existing regulations on the corporations' operations. In the summer of 2007, OFHEO adjusted the lending standards that applied to the two corporations so that they could buy up to $40 billion worth of new sub-prime loans. In February 2008, the Bush administration pushed an economic stimulus bill through Congress that, among other things, increased the caps on the size of mortgages Fannie Mae and Freddie Mac were permitted to buy from loans worth $417,000 to those up to $729,000 in value. In March 2008, OFHEO lowered the amount of surplus capital that Fannie Mae had to hold above the statutory minimum requirement from 30 to 20 per cent, a condition which it had imposed as part of the accounting settlement in 2004. This change effectively provided Fannie Mae with the capacity to purchase another $200 billion worth of mortgages and mortgage-backed securities. Two months later, it reduced the surplus capital requirement at Fannie Mae again to 15 per cent. The cumulative consequences of these looser regulatory changes allowed the two corporations to expand significantly their lending and purchases. With much other mortgage lending exhausted, during 2008 Fannie Mae and Freddie Mac guaranteed around three-quarters of new mortgages.

However, in using Fannie Mae and Freddie Mac to try to resurrect the mortgage market, the Bush administration was relying on corporations that by the summer of 2008 were probably insolvent at prevailing market prices using mark-to-market accounting. They had huge liabilities and they were not in a position to sell off mortgage-backed securities from their investment portfolios because the market for these securities was dead. Whilst it was domestically utterly untenable for the Bush administration to let Fannie Mae and Freddie Mac fall because almost everything of what was left of the American mortgage market would have gone with them, by the summer of 2008 the options open in finding a way to save the two corporations had severely diminished. The Bear Stearns' crisis in March 2008 had damaged investor confidence in other financial corporations and the spreads on Fannie Mae and Freddie Mac's bonds over Treasuries rose to a 22-year high in the days before the Federal Reserve forced the sale of the investment bank.

Yet despite the rise in the cost of their borrowing, the two corporations were still able to procure credit from abroad through the second quarter of 2008 and indeed, as the spread over Treasury bonds increased in the wake of the Bear Stearns' crisis, so did the willingness of those states accumulating Fannie Mae and Freddie Mae's long-term securities as part of their foreign exchange reserves to purchase them. As Table 5.3 shows, foreign investors bought almost twice as many of these securities in June 2008 as they had in the first month of that year.

However, this aggregate purchase data hid the fact that since the beginning of 2008 some central banks had lost confidence in the debt issued by the two corporations. Although the east Asian central banks had continued to lend through the first half of 2008, the Russian Central Bank had retreated, reducing its holdings of Fannie Mae and Freddie Mac by 50 per cent between January and June 2008.[16]

*Table 5.3* Monthly net purchases of long-term agency bonds in billions of dollars, January–June 2008

| | **Total purchases by foreigners** | **Official foreign purchases** |
|---|---|---|
| January | 15.7 | –7.3 |
| February | 33.6 | 1.2 |
| March | 16.1 | 15.9 |
| April | 12.2 | 11 |
| May | 25.5 | 11 |
| June | 29.4 | 9.1 |

*Source*: United States Department of the Treasury, Monthly reports of cross-border financial flows, January–June 2008.

Crucially, from the end of June 2008, Russian anxiety spread. In July 2008, the share prices of the two corporations plunged and the price of credit default swaps on the bonds rose on suspicions of their insolvency. This time, the corporations' ability to raise money from abroad evaporated. Whilst in June 2008 foreigners had bought $29.4 billion of long-term agency bond of which central banks bought $11 billion, in July all foreigners sold a net $42 billion of which central banks relinquished $16.1 billion.

The crisis at Fannie Mae and Freddie Mac in July 2008 posed four enormous potential problems that crossed the whole financial relationship between the United States and east Asia. First, any escalation of the selling by foreign private investors and central banks risked a rout of the dollar; and indeed, by the end of the first week

*Table 5.4* Net monthly purchases of US agency bonds by foreigners in billions of dollars, May–August 2008

| | **Total purchases by foreigners** | **Official foreign purchases** |
|---|---|---|
| May | 25.5 | 11 |
| June | 29.4 | 9.1 |
| July | –42 | –16.1 |
| August | –24. 2 | –13.1 |

*Source*: United States Department of the Treasury, Monthly reports of cross-border financial flows, May–August 2008.

of July, the problems at the corporations, and the fear that the government would have to bail them out, had weakened the dollar further.[17] Second, if the American government did have to rescue or nationalise Fannie Mae and Freddie Mac it would have to accept absorbing huge liabilities at a time when a significant rise in the budget deficit was already inevitable because of the fiscal stimulus bills enacted that year. In April 2008, Standard and Poor's had warned that if the government had to rescue the two corporations it could lose its triple A-rating.[18] Any such scenario was likely to produce more dollar weakness and increase the fear of the east Asian states about the medium- to long-term cost of maintaining their financial relationship with the United States. Third, as yields on the two corporations' bonds rose as foreign creditors' confidence drained away so did the rate on 30-year mortgages when cutting interest rates was a domestic political imperative in the United States. If the Federal Reserve now had to reduce the discount rate further to get mortgage interest rates down again, the monetary rewards for the east Asian side of lending would diminish further and the risk of more dollar depreciation would be accentuated.

Fourth, whilst the Asian stock markets had hitherto remained relatively immune from the fall in share prices that had hit the financial sectors in the United States and Europe, in the summer of 2008 they suffered as investors worried that any losses on Fannie Mae and Freddie Mac would hurt Asian banks as well.[19] The Chinese state-owned commercial bank, the Bank of China, one of the country's largest foreign exchange lenders, later said that, as of the end of September 2008, it had held $6.2 billion of debt issued by Fannie Mae and Freddie Mac and $3.8 billion worth of mortgage-backed securities guaranteed by them.[20] Between June and August 2008, Bank of China reduced its holdings of the two corporations' bonds and securities by $4.6 billion.[21] China Construction Bank, another of the state-owned commercial banks, said in the autumn of 2008 that it held $1.5 billion of securities of one kind or another.[22] Bloomberg calculated that in early September 2008 Chinese banks had collectively around $20 billion in the corporations' bonds and securities.[23] The Japanese banks were also exposed. As of March 2008, Bloomberg similarly estimated that Japan's three largest banks had $45 billion of bonds and securities issued by Fannie Mae and Freddie Mac.[24] In these circumstances, if the two corporations were not to be rescued by the

American government, then the Chinese and Japanese banking sectors would be vulnerable exactly to the kind of problems already afflicting American and European banks. Any such development could only add to the financial and monetary burdens that the economic relationship with the United States now imposed on the two states.

The withdrawal of Fannie Mae and Freddie Mac's foreign creditors left the Bush administration with effectively no policy autonomy. International economic realities required it to accept that there was no alternative but to offer financial support to the two corporations. On 13 July, the Treasury Secretary, Hank Paulson, asked Congress for new authority for the Treasury to buy unspecified amounts of the shares and debt of the corporations and for the just-established Federal Housing Finance Agency to take the two corporations into conservatorship if it deemed that necessary. The Federal Reserve also announced that the corporations could borrow from it. To give the Treasury the capacity to offer this scale of financial support Congress also had legally to raise the national debt ceiling by $800 billion. Explaining the administration's decision, James Lockhart, the Director of the Federal Housing Finance Agency, later told the House Financial Services Committee that the two corporations could no longer raise and maintain capital:

> In particular, the capacity to raise capital to absorb further losses without Treasury department support vanished. That left both enterprises unable to provide counter-cyclical market support. Worse, it threatened to further damage the mortgage and housing markets if they had to sell assets.[25]

In an interview with Bloomberg, Paulson made clear that this announcement of support was a decision brought about by external constraints as much as any domestic consideration:

> I clearly talked with the Chinese through this. They've worked with me enough that they knew I wouldn't say it unless I believed it.[26]

Paulson's announcement allowed Freddie Mac to raise $3 billion in short-term bonds on 14 July albeit at a high spread over Treasury bonds. But the burst of investor confidence that made that issue possible was very short-lived. The following day, Moody's downgraded the corporations' credit ratings and the Securities and Exchange Commission restricted short selling of their shares.[27] During the second half of the month and into August, the corporations' share prices continued to plummet, the spread over Treasury bonds widened, and private and central bank investors continued to sell. On 29 August, the Bank of China said that it had significantly reduced its holdings of Fannie Mae and Freddie Mac's bonds and securities, and Fannie Mae's share price ended a six-day rally with a 14 per cent fall.[28] By the end of August, the Federal Reserve's custody data showed that there had been net selling of agency bonds for six consecutive weeks.[29] The two corporations had recorded net losses of around $15 billion over the previous four quarters, they were paying a higher spread over Treasury bonds than ever before, and their share values were down by more than 90 per cent in share value from the beginning of the year.[30]

By the beginning of September 2008, it was clear that the Bush administration's actions to try to resolve the crisis had failed. Critically, both corporations had imminent, substantial interest payments to make during the month and neither was in a position to make them. Through the preceding weeks, anxiety about what the American government would do next had mounted in east Asia. On 22 August, a former adviser to China's central bank, Yu Yongding, had warned:

> If the U.S. government allows Fannie and Freddie to fail and international investors are not compensated adequately, the consequences will be catastrophic. If it is not the end of the world, it is the end of the current international financial system. The seriousness of such failures could be beyond the stretch of people's imagination.[31]

Yet in reality the constraints of the economic relationship with the east Asian states on the United States, once again, left the Bush administration with no broad alternative. If Fannie Mae and Freddie Mac were allowed to default, east Asian support for the dollar would be terminated, and the whole international economy was likely to unravel with the shock, in addition to what was left of the American mortgage market and the balance sheets of the banks holding the two corporations' bonds and securities.

Over the first weekend of September, the Federal Housing Finance Agency asked the Federal Reserve Board and the Office of Comptroller of the Currency to examine the two corporations' books. Between them they concluded that Fannie Mae and Freddie Mac had inadequate capital. The scrutiny revealed that as well as being extremely highly leveraged, as was already known, the two corporations had counted deferred tax credits, which could be deducted from taxes on future profits, as capital held under minimum capital requirements. In Fannie Mae's case, these tax credits represented more than 40 per cent of what it was counting for the capital requirement and in Freddie Mac's case more than 50 per cent. As Dallas Federal Reserve President said afterwards: 'we concluded that the capital of these institutions was too low in relation to their exposure ... and that capital in and of itself was of low quality'.[32] The same weekend the undersecretary for international affairs at the Treasury, David McCormick, called foreign central banks and foreign commercial banks to tell them that the government would protect the bonds and securities issued by the two corporations and other Treasury officials held briefing meetings with Chinese representatives.[33] According to some of those present, the Chinese officials questioned every detail of what the Treasury proposed to do.[34]

On 7 September 2008, the Federal Housing Finance Agency took Fannie Mae and Freddie Mac into conservatorship. The conservatorship wiped out existing shareholders and guaranteed all the bonds and securities held by creditors. In a joint press conference, James Lockhart and Hank Paulson said that each corporation would have access to up to $100 billion of Treasury money to cover losses, and the Treasury would begin to buy mortgage-backed securities from them. In return, the Treasury was to receive $1 billion of preferred stock and would receive $100 million a year as a dividend. The terms of the conservatorship allowed Fannie Mae and Freddie Mac to increase modestly their mortgage-backed securities portfolios until December 2009 when they had to fall by 10 per cent a year until they reached a value of $250 billion. Each was expected, by contrast, to increase significantly its mortgage lending. However, trying to draw this distinction between the 'good' and 'bad activities of the corporations quickly proved problematic. Forcing a curtailment of Fannie Mae and Freddie Mac's mortgage-backed securities purchases could in the circumstances only inflict more harm on the mortgage market. The systemic risk that the investment portfolios posed had already come to pass and the government had responded by making the corporations' liabilities its own. In this context, just a month after the conservatorship announcement, the Federal Housing Finance Agency reversed course on the investment portfolios and told the two corporations to buy $20 billion of largely sub-prime and Alt-A mortgage-backed securities a month.[35]

In explaining and justifying the federal government's takeover of Fannie Mae and Freddie Mac, Paulson was explicit about the reality of the domestic and external imperatives that had left the administration with no politically realistic alternative but to act as it did. At the initial press conference, he stressed the domestic side of the problem:

> I have long said that the housing correction poses the biggest risk to our economy. It is a drag on our economic growth, and at the heart of the turmoil and stress for our financial markets and financial institutions. Our economy and our markets will not recover until the bulk of this housing correction is behind us. Fannie Mae and Freddie Mac are critical to turning the corner on housing. Therefore, the primary mission of these enterprises now will be to proactively work to increase the availability of mortgage finance.[36]

But in later interviews, Paulson admitted that the growing concern of foreign investors about the two corporations was one of the reasons for acting:

> There was definitely concern overseas. [Foreign investors] have reduced their level of buying and some had stopped buying and there was some selling. ... This was just obvious.[37]

He also acknowledged that successive administrations and Congress were responsible for generating the expectations of creditors that had now had to be met, whatever the ultimate cost to the federal government:

> Because the U.S. government created these ambiguities, we have a responsibility to both avert and ultimately address the systemic risk now posed by the scale and breadth of the holdings.[38]

Since, he further argued, American politicians had brought this problem upon themselves, they now had to ensure that in the future the

American state has a very different kind of relationship with the two mortgage corporations than the one that had prevailed for the previous four decades:

> The new Congress and the next Administration must decide what role government in general, and these entities in particular, should play in the housing market. There is a consensus today that these enterprises pose a systemic risk and they cannot continue in their current form. Government support needs to be either explicit or non-existent, and structured to resolve the conflict between public and private purposes. And policymakers must address the issue of systemic risk. ... We will make a grave error if we don't use this time out to permanently address the structural issues presented by the government-sponsored enterprises.[39]

Whilst just what that relationship might be was likely to provoke a heated political debate within the United States of the kind that had run through the battle over regulation, it was this time unlikely to take place with so little reference to the international conditions that had allowed Fannie Mae and Freddie Mac to become the corporations they had.

## The aftermath: The continuing drain of external confidence

The week after the federal rescue of Fannie Mae and Freddie Mac, the financial crisis took a dramatic deleterious turn. Over the weekend of 13–14 September, the Treasury and Federal Reserve decided to let the investment bank Lehman Brothers file for bankruptcy. In the following days stock markets around the world took huge losses and the money market funds and commercial paper markets stopped functioning. In the financial turmoil that ensued over the next weeks, the Bush administration orchestrated the sale of Merrill Lynch to Bank of America, effectively nationalised AIG and brought about the conversion of the investment banks Goldman Sachs and Morgan Stanley into bank holding companies. Meanwhile the Federal Deposit Insurance Corporation seized control of Washington Mutual, the largest savings and loan association in the country and transferred most of its assets to JP Morgan and unsuccessfully tried to organise and subsidise the acquisition of Wachovia, a large commercial bank, by

Citigroup. Across Europe governments took to similar huge-scale state intervention to try to rescue their own financial sectors. With the prospect of imminent meltdown in banking sectors throughout the western world, the Bush administration also asked Congress to pass emergency legislation, authorising the Treasury to buy up to $700 billion worth of toxic assets, including mortgage-backed securities held by banks in what it called a Troubled Asset Relief Programme (TARP). In early October 2008, after the House of Representatives had voted down the original bill, precipitating a large fall in the Dow Jones in a matter of minutes, Congress passed the Emergency Economic Stabilisation Act establishing TARP.

The escalation of the financial crisis in the middle of September 2008 and the response of the Bush administration to it changed the consequences of what the Federal Housing Finance Agency had done in placing Fannie Mae and Freddie Mac into federal conservatorship. In wiping out the existing shareholders, the government had hurt several large banks, including a number of regional banks and Citigroup, which held preferred shares and had to make more write-downs on top of what were already large losses. Whilst Paulson tried to downplay these losses, saying that the conservatorship would only have significant consequences for a few banks, the American Bankers Association reported that nearly a third of American banks held preferred stock in Fannie Mae and Freddie Mac and that their average exposure relative to their equity capital was 11 per cent.[40] Whilst the federal government's rescue of the two corporations saved the American mortgage and mortgage-backed securities market from complete collapse, it also spread problems in a different way through the domestic banking sector.

Meanwhile, in assuming responsibilities for Fannie Mae and Freddie Mac's collective $5.4 trillion liabilities in debt and mortgage-backed securities, the Bush administration had doubled the American state's total debt. In the few days after the announcement of the conservatorship, credit default swaps on Treasury bonds hit their highest ever level. By the end of September 2008, the burden of honouring those liabilities if necessary had been deepened by the amount of money the government had implicitly committed itself to borrow to pay for TARP and provide financial support to AIG. To compound matters, the size of the fiscal commitments of the American state made re-establishing the creditworthiness of Fannie Mae and Freddie Mac very difficult. In the first days after the state takeover of the two corporations, representatives of several of the east Asian central banks said publicly that they were reassured that the bonds and securities that they held would be honoured. The Governor of the Bank of Japan, Masaaki Shirakawa, said that he expected the takeover to 'stabilise' American and global financial markets, whilst the Chinese governor, Zhou Xiaochuan, described the move as 'positive'.[41] More strongly, the Taiwan Deputy premier, Paul Chiu, declared:

> [It is] a very important measure. This does not relieve us completely, but it will help stabilise world financial markets.[42]

However, east Asian confidence was seriously damaged. As one Chinese government official said: 'Confidence has not yet been restored in this market so Chinese banks are going to take a wait and see attitude and not buy any more [Fannie and Freddie] debt.'[43] The chief economist of China International Investment Corp, China's largest investment bank, remarked that 'th[e] crisis will likely lead to greater diversification of foreign-exchange reserve investments'.[44] And where it most mattered, in the debt markets for Fannie Mae and Freddie Mac's bonds, there was no reversal by the east Asian states. For the rest of September and October, the central banks continued to make net sales of the two corporations' bonds and securities.

Whilst the Bush administration had appeared to hope that the public terms of the conservatorship and a private tacit understanding that the American government would ensure that timely interests payments were made would be sufficient to restore external creditor confidence and re-establish access to capital for the corporations, they were not. The only remaining, realistic alternative open to the Bush administration to shift the risk-judgement being made by the corporations was to make the American state legally responsible for Fannie Mae and Freddie Mac's liabilities. This, however, would have required action by Congress and would have formally added to the national debt at a time when market confidence in the American state's long-term ability to service that debt was diminishing. Put differently, the Bush administration could have eliminated the spread on the two corporations' debt over Treasury bonds and helped the mortgage market in doing so, but it could have done so only at the price of raising the cost for the American state of issuing long-term debt. It chose to maintain the *status quo* rather than ask Congress to act. In late October 2006, James Lockhart tried to reassure investors, saying publicly that the two corporations had 'access to credit from the US Treasury' (and) there was 'an explicit guarantee to existing and future debt holders of Fannie Mae and Freddie Mac'.[45] But the two corporations' foreign creditors continued to sell. Between October and December 2008, foreign private investors and central banks made net sales of more than $100 billion worth of the corporations' long-term securities. As Table 5.5 shows, even when some external confidence returned on long-term Treasury bonds and corporate bonds in December 2008, it did not on Fannie Mae and Freddie Mac's securities.

*Table 5.5* Official and private net purchases of various long-term American securities in billions of dollars, September–December 2008

| | Private agency bonds | Official agency bonds | Private Treasury bonds | Official Treasury bonds | Private corporate bonds | Official corporate bonds |
|---|---|---|---|---|---|---|
| September | 14.8 | –8.7 | 15.8 | 4.9 | –7.3 | –1.2 |
| October | –35.5 | –16.7 | 3.4 | –1.1 | –13.8 | 0.7 |
| November | –10.9 | –11.6 | 0.4 | –26.2 | –15.3 | –0.9 |
| December | –24.6 | –12.9 | 11.1 | 3.9 | 37.5 | 3.5 |

*Source*: United States Department of the Treasury, Monthly reports of cross-border financial flows, September–December 2008.

The Bush administration was unable to restore much external confidence in Fannie Mae and Freddie Mac because after the onset of the post-Lehman bankruptcy phase of the financial crisis foreign central banks, foreign investors, and the east Asian states in particular, became significantly risk averse. In the last two months of 2008, the only dollar assets foreign central banks were interested in purchasing in any large volume were short-term Treasury bills, which were the least risky debt on the market.

*Table 5.6* Official net monthly purchases of short-term Treasury bonds in billions of dollars, September–December 2008

| | Purchases |
|---|---|
| September | 31.2 |
| October | 83.8 |
| November | 66.6 |
| December | 30.7 |

*Source*: United States Department of the Treasury, Monthly reports of cross-border financial flows, September–December 2008.

For no state was this truer than for China. On 3 December 2008, the chairman of China's sovereign wealth fund, said that the CIC would not invest in any more western financial companies, declaring:

> Right now we don't have the courage to invest in financial institutions because we don't know what problems we will put ourselves into.[46]

The same day, the Chinese Vice-Premier, Wang Qishan, said after a meeting between the Chinese and American Treasuries:

> I hope the United States will take all necessary measures to stabilise its economy and financial markets as soon as possible and to ensure the security of Chinese investments and interests in the United States.[47]

In February 2008, the chief fund investor for the Japanese conglomerate, Mitsubishi, said that Asian investors would not buy any more bonds issued by Fannie Mae and Freddie Mac until they carried an explicit American government guarantee because the risk was otherwise too great.[48] In sum, by early 2009, there was no longer a basis for further east Asian financial support for Fannie Mae and Freddie Mac's commercial operations despite the fact that the corporations were under the control of the American state.

In the absence of the foreign funds that had proved so crucial over the previous few years, the interest rate at which the two corporations could lend remained the same as it had been before the Bush administration had made their debt the responsibility of the American state. To change this, the Federal Reserve and the Treasury had to act themselves to provide domestic financial support. In November 2008, the Federal Reserve President, Ben Bernanke, said that the government might need to back mortgages indefinitely to prevent serious damage to the housing market in any future financial crisis.[49] The same month Freddie Mac asked to take nearly $14 billion of the money to which it had access under the terms of the conservatorship after it announced a third quarterly loss of more than $25 billion. For its part, Fannie Mae made a third quarter loss of $29 billion and said that it might need more than the $100 billion the government had already allocated to it.[50] Meanwhile the Bush administration announced that the Treasury would be buying up to

$500 billion worth of the mortgage-backed securities issued or guaranteed by Fannie Mae and Freddie Mac and up to $100 billion of each of the corporations' bonds. These purchases began in December and finally produced a reduction in the spread on the corporations' securities over Treasury bonds. With that reduction came a fall in interest rates on 30-year mortgages to their lowest level in four years. Nonetheless, without access to new foreign capital, Fannie Mae and Freddie Mac remained in a financially precarious position and the imperative for the American government to extend more state support remained unabated. In February 2009, the Obama administration said that it was doubling the amount of capital available to each of the two corporations to $400 million and raised the cap on their investment portfolios. At the end of the following month, after both corporations reported enormous losses for the fourth quarter of 2008, the Treasury gave $30.8 billion to Freddie Mac and $15.2 billion to Fannie Mae.

## Conclusions

The economic relationship between the United States and east Asia helped to make the sub-prime boom possible and the structural weakness of the dollar, which had become the essential economic vulnerability of the relationship, played a part, via the rise in interest rates from the second half of 2004, in creating the conditions in which that boom unravelled and the worst financial crisis since the inter-war years began. During most of the first phase of the financial crisis – that period from the summer of 2007 to the spring of 2008 – the interdependencies created by the Pacific economic relationship, saved the American financial sector and provided support for the Bush administration's attempt to rescue the mortgage market through Fannie Mae and Freddie Mac. The second phase of the financial crisis – that period which began with the Treasury and Federal Reserve Board's moves to force the sale of Bear Stearns and which ended with the federal takeover of Fannie Mae and Freddie Mac – arose in large part because the east Asian governments decided to change the terms on which they had hitherto operated in the relationship. They continued to buy dollar assets and in doing so supported the American currency, but they henceforth discriminated more sharply between the assets they trusted and those they deemed a risk. More particularly, the Chinese government decided not to let its sovereign wealth fund inject capital into any more American investment banks, and the east Asian central banks declined to provide any more cheap credit to Fannie Mae and Freddie Mac. In doing the latter, they showed themselves unwilling to take *de facto* financial responsibility for the attempt by the American government to rescue the American mortgage market. As a result, the American state had to take upon itself the direct burden of providing money to that market. Having done that, the Bush administration almost immediately found itself deciding to take responsibility for significant parts of the broader financial sector too, as the financial crisis entered its post-Lehman bankruptcy third phase.

In accumulating potentially huge financial liabilities in the final four months of 2008, the American government had reinforced some of the most acute difficulties that had emerged in the Pacific economic relationship. With the east Asian states less confident about the political will in the United States to honour foreign investments and liabilities than ever before, they now would have to act as at least the creditor of last resort for a very large American budget deficit. If they were not willing to do that, and private purchases of American Treasury bonds were not forthcoming, they risked a dollar crisis. But if they were to continue to act as the creditor of last resort, they would have to add to the risks that their huge portfolios of dollar reserves already imposed on them. A ballooning American federal borrowing requirement made the economic relationship between the United States and east Asia more fraught than ever, however tightly economic interdependence held the relationship together in the short term.

# 6
# Conclusions

By early 2009, the economic relationship between the United States and east Asia was first and foremost defined by the financial relationship between the United States and China. Putting together the holdings of the Chinese central bank, the state-owned banks, and China's sovereign wealth fund, Brad Setser and Arpanda Pandey have estimated that in early 2009 China held foreign assets of about \$2.3 trillion, the equivalent of more than 50 per cent of China's GDP. Around 70 per cent of these assets were denominated in dollars.[1] During 2008, China provided more than 50 per cent of the capital flows required to finance the American current account deficit, and by that year's end China was holding about twice as many foreign exchange reserves as Japan.[2]

Whilst the general economic relationship between the United States and east Asia that developed after the Asian financial crisis initially satisfied a set of mutual interests, by 2009 the US-China financial relationship was one increasingly dominated by the risks produced by the consequences of past interdependence and the fear they induced. Today, China's economy is far more exposed to its portfolios of dollar holdings than it was even in 2006 when the Chinese leadership had begun to accept some appreciation of the yuan. For its part, the American state is responsible for servicing far more debt than it was when the federal government's borrowing last peaked. A large proportion of that debt had arisen because the American state was eventually forced to mop up the consequences of the vast flows of capital across the Pacific over much of the previous decade. The American state also now has direct responsibility for two huge mortgage corporations around which the whole mortgage sector of the American economy depends, and these corporations have massive liabilities. When the Asian central banks forsook the debt of Fannie Mae and Freddie Mac, first the American government had to step in and guarantee those bonds and securities, and then the Federal Reserve had to take the medium- to long-term inflationary risk of buying up their debt. This did nothing to advance confidence in the east Asian states in the security of their dollar investments. As a result of this loss of east Asian faith, the still large American balance of payments deficit was primarily being financed by early 2009 on a precarious, short-term basis.

## Interdependence as fear: China's burden

The post-2008 economic relationship between the United States and China leaves each state vulnerable to rather different degrees. The Chinese leadership is self-consciously operating under a host of overt and acute international constraints. China's fundamental problem is the sheer scale of its exposure to the risk of substantial depreciation of the American currency. This risk had already grown every year that China had added to its dollar's portfolio, but the large increase in the American government's borrowing in 2008 significantly exacerbated the risk because it is likely to put more medium- to long-term structural downward pressure on the dollar. On top of its near-certain future currency loss, China, by 2009, had lost billions of dollars on its reserves through its diversification into equities after it established the China Investment Corporation (CIC). The Chinese leadership was also badly burned by a set of misjudgements about how the American government would act towards China's American investments. It had not expected the American government to take over Washington Mutual in which China's State Administration of Foreign Exchange had invested.[3] Reportedly, it was also dismayed by the Bush administration's decision to let Lehman Brothers go, especially as the CIC had a $5.4 billion investment in a money-market fund that collapsed as a result of the investment bank's bankruptcy. By early 2009, the Chinese government had decided that the various Chinese state investment agencies should stay away from dollar assets carrying even the semblance of risk. The investment agencies were now buying neither Fannie Mae and Freddie Mac's securities nor other corporate bonds and equities, nor long-term Treasury securities. In investing this way at a moment when American monetary policy was exceptionally expansive, China was left effectively purchasing only assets that yielded virtually no interest. Whilst the purchase of short-term Treasury bonds mitigated the risk of any immediate dollar crisis, and provides a quick exit option if and when one were to develop, it also ensured that China was left with nothing in the short term to compensate for its inevitable long-term currency losses.

China's chief gain from the economic relationship to the United States prior to the events of 2008 had been the support that it provided via the exchange rate for export-led growth. Yet the onset of the third phase of the financial crisis destroyed, at least in the short term, the trade opportunity that interdependence had hitherto sustained. In the final quarter of 2008, east Asian exports, including China's, collapsed spectacularly. Between January 2008 and January 2009, South Korea's exports fell by 33 per cent, and between December 2007 and December 2008, Taiwan's fell by 42 per cent. Between February 2008 and February 2009, Japanese exports fell by nearly 50 per cent and China's by 43 per cent. These falls precipitated large drops in east Asian industrial production and GDP. In the fourth quarter of 2008, GDP fell in Thailand by 22 per cent, in South Korea by 21 per cent, and in Japan by 12 per cent. By February 2009, Japan's industrial production was falling at a year-on-year rate of 38 per cent. Whilst China's economy continued to grow through the final quarter of 2008, it did so at a rate several points below that which the Chinese government has long considered safe for employment purposes.

The fallout of the financial crisis for China's exports also raised perhaps a more fundamental problem for China because it sharply exposed the general vulnerabilities of export-driven economies under conditions of interdependence. The falls in national growth in late 2008 and early 2009 across the world were considerably higher in east Asia than in the United States or much of Europe, and even within western Europe, the strongest-exporting economy, Germany, suffered a particularly deep decline. When the east Asian economies did begin to recover in the second quarter of 2009, they did so in response to large domestic fiscal stimuli rather than exports.[4] This susceptibility of exports to a worldwide fall in demand reinforced the increasingly intractable dilemma China faced in choosing between the markedly conflicting international imperatives on the financial and trade issues that the economic relationship with the United States had created. Moreover, by 2009, the cost of evading any decisive choice between moving the burden of growth to domestic demand, and accepting future currency losses in doing so, and satisfying the immediate interests of export competitiveness was higher than ever before. The shock the financial crisis had wrought on export-dependent sectors of the economy left the Chinese government with every short-term reason to try to stop any yuan appreciation at all against the dollar to contain the damage to trade, but to do that the Chinese central bank was likely to have to purchase yet more assets that carried a significant medium- to long-term currency risk.

In practice, the Chinese government tried to face both ways. By the end of 2008, it had restored an effective peg against the dollar to stop the yuan appreciating any further. It was also directing state-banks to lend more to exporters, providing tax rebates to the export sector, and preparing to provide credit support for exports. In December 2008, Li Yizhong, the minister of industry and information technology, publicly said that China would 'resort to tariff and trade policies to facilitate export of labour-intensive and core technology-supported industries'.[5] Meanwhile, the Chinese government was also looking for ways to shift the medium-term emphasis of its development strategy from export-led growth to domestic consumption.[6] By the end of 2008, it had significantly increased expenditure on education, health, social security, and employment.[7] When the Chinese economy, along with the others in east Asia, started to recover from the financial crisis in the second quarter of 2009, the increase in growth came entirely from domestic demand and exports continued to fall.[8] Each approach had its limitations. The short-term, nationalist reaction to the problem was bound to antagonise Washington and, indeed, in December 2008, the American government filed a case at the World Trade Organisation, alleging that China was providing illegal subsidies to exporters. Nonetheless, to make a decisive strategic shift away from export-led growth would require accepting an appreciation of the yen and facing up to future currency losses sooner rather than later.[9]

Meanwhile, the Chinese leadership's political difficulties with the economic relationship had become more overt. The fallout of the financial crisis produced a domestic political problem for the Chinese leadership. China's losses on its American investments drew a string of criticism from influential economic commentators. One editorial in a government-owned newspaper pronounced that the '[United States] should not expect [a] continuous inflow of more cheap foreign capital to fund its one-after-another massive bailouts'.[10] In late 2008, a fast circulating internet essay attacked the Chinese central bank for 'collud[ing] with Henry Paulson to buy US bonds, forc[ing] [yuan] appreciation, attach[ing] China's economy to the U.S. and break[ing] China's economic independence'.[11]

The ferocity of the domestic censure meant that the Chinese leadership could not simply deal in a practical and pragmatic way with the American government on the complex economic issues that existed between them. It rhetorically had to appease domestic critics in its public utterances on any aspect of the economic relationship with the United States whilst, at the same time, it had to try to ensure that in doing so it did not provoke the Americans into any new protectionist action. In February 2009, a senior official at China's Banking Regulatory Commission was reported as saying:

> We hate you guys. Once you start issuing $1 trillion–$2 trillion ... we know the dollar is going to depreciate, so we hate you guys but there is nothing much we can do. ... Compared with gold or bonds issued by other countries and regions, US Treasury bonds are still an option [for China]. But if the US government issues a large amount of Treasury bonds amid efforts to deal with the economic crisis, all investors who hold US Treasuries will suffer losses.[12]

One month later, the Chinese Premier Wen Jiabo, in less dramatic language, urged the United States to take action to guarantee its 'good credit', saying he was worried about the 'safety' of China's holdings of American government debt:

> We have lent huge amounts of money to the United States. Of course we are concerned about the safety of our assets. To be honest, I am a little bit worried. I request the US to maintain its good credit, to honour its promises and to guarantee the safety of China's assets.[13]

During the same month the Chinese central bank governor, Zhou Xiaochuan, published an essay arguing that the existing international monetary and financial order was fundamentally flawed:

> The outbreak of the current crisis and its spill-over in the world have confronted us with a long-existing but still unanswered

> question, ie what kind of international reserve currency do we need to secure global financial stability and facilitate world economic growth.[14]

He called for a new reserve currency to replace the dollar:

> The desirable goal of reforming the international monetary system, therefore, is to create an international reserve currency that is disconnected from individual nations and is able to remain stable in the long run, thus removing the inherent deficiencies caused by using credit-based national currencies. ... A super-sovereign reserve currency managed by a global institution could be used to both create and control the global liquidity. And when a country's currency is no longer used as the yardstick for global trade and as the benchmark for other currencies, the exchange rate policy of the country would be far more effective in adjusting economic imbalances. This will significantly reduce the risks of a future crisis and enhance crisis management capability.[15]

The Chinese central bank will certainly have known that American Presidents would not voluntarily accede to the eclipse of the dollar as the primary reserve currency in the world in this way. Even more importantly, during the first months of 2009, China appeared actually to increase its holdings of short-term Treasury bonds despite this confrontational rhetoric.[16] Nonetheless, Zhou seemed to have wanted to make the American government understand the depth of the Chinese leadership's unease at the position China had found itself and the domestic problem for China that each side's actions have created. Given the fact that thus far China has not been prepared even to disclose information about the nature of its reserves to the International Monetary Fund (IMF), Zhou's suggestion that China might be prepared to internationalise its dollar reserve problem indicated just how much of a burden the leadership believed the financial relationship with the United States now imposed:

> Compared with separate management of reserves by individual countries, the centralized management of part of the global reserve by a trustworthy international institution with a reasonable return to encourage participation will be more effective in deterring speculation and stabilizing financial markets. ... With

> its universal membership, its unique mandate of maintaining monetary and financial stability, and as an international 'supervisor' on the macroeconomic policies of its member countries, the IMF, equipped with its expertise, is endowed with a natural advantage to act as the manager of its member countries' reserves.

For its part, the United States faces fewer immediate constraints than China but, nonetheless, has less policy autonomy than it did earlier in the decade. Although, over the past few years, two Presidents and Congress have massively increased American government borrowing, it is not clear that the Obama administration at least perceives this debt as a constraint or something to fear. The President's first draft budget in 2009, and the proposals that contained for future expenditure projects particularly on healthcare, would suggest that the Obama administration is not overly worried about a sharp increase in federal borrowing, despite lofty rhetoric to the contrary. A preliminary report from the Congressional Budget Office calculated that the deficit for 2009 would be 11.9 per cent based on existing fiscal commitments and 13.1 per cent if Obama's draft budget were to be enacted whilst the cumulative deficit for the years 2010 to 2019 on the basis would be $9.3 trillion, more than twice the baseline projecting from 2008. Meanwhile, the Congressional Budget Office warned, the national debt would rise from 41 per cent of GDP in 2008 to 82 per cent in 2019 and the net interest payments would add $1 trillion to the deficit.[17]

Certainly, the United States' dependence on China as a creditor for much of the past decade has alarmed some in the American Congress and prompted some domestic political discussion. In 2004, Robert Byrd, the Senate's longest serving member declared:

> It's great political rhetoric to claim that America doesn't have to ask the permission of other nations to defend itself or do anything else for that matter, but when we rely so heavily on other nations to pay our way in the world, our haughty claims of independence are just so much bluff. Unfortunately the rest of the world knows what we will not admit. We are beholden to foreigners to pay our way.[18]

Meanwhile, on the night of the Wisconsin Democratic party primary in 2008, Hillary Clinton attacked the Bush administration for allowing the United States to become financially dependent on China and pronounced that dependency was now a constraint on American foreign policy:

> And while you pinch pennies to stay within your budget, the President blew the bank on tax breaks for his friends and no-bid contracts for his cronies, borrowing hundreds of billions of dollars from China to pay for it all. He has signed a sub-prime mortgage on America's economic future and that's your future. And so when people ask me 'why can't we get tough on China?' well, when was the last time you got tough on your banker? And so we have to get back to fiscal responsibility in order to get tough on China because we shouldn't be borrowing so much money from them.[19]

Looked at from a historical perspective, there are some reasons to suppose that rising government debt is likely to reduce the autonomy of the American state over time, not just economically but conceivably militarily too. Several previous great powers have been undone by the political fallout of borrowing, whether from domestic or foreign creditors, such that an internal debt crisis had led to external defeat or decline. The United Provinces, 17th century Spain, and *ancien régime* France are in many ways the classic cases of this historical pattern. At a general level, there are three possible difficult scenarios for indebted states: external creditors can use access to future credit as leverage for a political or military purpose against them; debtor states can find themselves in a fiscal position where they cannot repay; and creditors can lose confidence that the debtor state will repay in the future and, consequently, refuse to lend any more money. Internationally powerful states, like the United States, have historically proved more liable to run into the second and third of these problems than the first. However, they have done so not because of the absolute volume of their borrowing in any instance, but either because they have exhausted alternative creditors, or because they have been unable for domestic political reasons to service their debt at a moderate cost in interest.

There is also no reason to suppose that rising government debt necessarily imposes constraints on internationally powerful states. The British state during the 18th and early 19th century borrowed significantly more than the French state. It not only avoided a debt-induced political crisis like the one that afflicted France in the summer of 1789, but it used its borrowing to finance its rise to become the dominant European power in the first half of the 19th century. It was able to do this because it maintained its creditors' confidence in its political capacity to raise future taxes to pay for the loans. Consequently, it could service its debt at half the rate of interest levied on France. By contrast, the United Provinces, Spain and *ancien régime* France all endured transformative debt crises because for domestic political reasons their debt became unserviceable. The government in the United Provinces provoked riots when, as its debt burden rose during war time, it tried to raise more taxes from its constituent provinces that enjoyed substantial fiscal autonomy. The Spanish crown's attempts to tax more to sustain borrowing during the Thirty Years' War produced similar revolts in Portugal and Catalonia. When the French crown needed new taxes to restore creditors' confidence in 1789, it was forced to summon the Estates-General, prompting the political crisis that destroyed the *ancien regime*. Historically, whether large-scale borrowing is problematic for internationally powerful states has been dependent on domestic political circumstances and how governments manage the problems that the political conditions of procuring credit bring.[20]

Today, states face the same basic fiscal problems as older states did: to pay for their expenditure they must either raise immediate revenue in taxes, or borrow and levy taxes later. However, they also face new problems that arise out of the interaction of their own borrowing and those of other economic agents, and these are generated by the relationships between current accounts, exchange rates, and private short-term international capital flows. By the standards of the 17th and 18th century great powers, the American federal government's debt is very low. Nonetheless, the future absolute burden of that debt is uncertain. The American Treasury is not in a position to know what the liabilities of the financial sector it is guaranteeing are, and it has never been capable of accurately calculating what they are likely to be in the future. Indeed, in the summer of 2007, the banks themselves had no idea just how badly damaged their balance sheets were and now governments everywhere have learned that those losses are on a scale that they would probably have thought inconceivable during the early months of the crisis.

Paradoxically, in this instance this problem matters in the short term less for the debtor state than the creditor. The uncertainty about the scale of future American liabilities and the probable impact on the foreign exchange markets of the necessity of more federal borrowing can only damage further the confidence of the Chinese leadership about the wisdom of sustaining the present terms of the economic relationship with the United States. It leaves the Chinese leadership unable to judge how much lending China might have to do in the future to support the American fiscal position. Moreover, it adds to the future losses that China will have to incur when it does change its exchange rate policy because it increases the likelihood of future dollar depreciation. Neither beyond radically reversing fiscal policy is there much the United States can do to reassure China. In the 1970s, the United States was fiscally constrained by the weakness of the dollar. Then, the Carter administration decided to sell debt known as 'Carter bonds' denominated in German marks and Swiss francs to fund its borrowing at a moment when its foreign creditors had lost confidence in American policy towards the dollar. Yet in the circumstances of the present international economy, it is difficult to see how the Chinese government would want the Americans to try anything akin to 'Carter bonds' because such a move would almost certainly lead to exactly the kind of dollar crisis that such an act would be conceived to avoid.

Nonetheless, that the United States is borrowing from a state that is not lending in its own currency is in the final instance a problem for the United States' autonomy as well as China's. The Chinese leadership does not have anything but an exceptionally painful way out if it were to lose confidence entirely in American creditworthiness. Nonetheless, the more uncertainty it has to navigate, the greater the risk for the United States that it will quite suddenly decide to change course and take the short-term hit on currency losses that it ultimately cannot avoid. Perhaps also the United States risks China beginning to look for more foreign policy leverage from its lending to compensate for its losses. Consequently, although the United States is significantly less constrained than most previous internationally powerful debtor states have been, no American government can afford to be that cavalier about what it expects China to absorb for the sake of an economic *status quo* that is hugely problematic as seen from Beijing. It is perhaps then not surprising that reports of the Strategic Economic Dialogue meeting in July 2009 between American and Chinese officials suggest that the Obama administration eschewed raising the subject of China's exchange rate policy, despite the fact that over the previous six months the yuan's real-trade weighted value had fallen by 8 per cent.[21] After a summit held between President Obama and the Chinese President, Hu Jintao, in Beijing in November 2009, Obama publicly expressed hope that China would move 'a more market-oriented exchange rate over time', but appeared to procure no practical concession from the Chinese leadership.[22]

Historical experience would suggest that the United States' future external creditworthiness turns on whether there is the domestic political basis to sustain the American government's present borrowing and, just as importantly, the judgement that the Chinese leadership makes about whether or not this is the case. This question goes beyond whether any President and Congress would be politically willing to increase taxes significantly in the medium term. It also matters whether the fact that American taxes will need to be raised to make interest payments specifically to China will in time become a politically contested issue. The Bush administration did succeed in acting to protect China and Japan's interests as major creditors to Fannie Mae and Freddie Mac without provoking a political crisis, despite wiping out domestic shareholders of the two corporations. More generally, American citizens appear to have directed their political anger about the financial crisis at Wall Street rather than other states. However, the United States' economic relationship with China has the potential to be politically very awkward for any President if contingently a dramatic issue rises to the surface at any time. In 2005, a vote in the House of Representatives forced a Chinese firm to withdraw its bid for a small American oil firm, and the remarks by Wen Jiabo in March 2009 might suggest that the Chinese leadership has some anxiety that there could be a repeat of such a scenario on a financial issue. Yet we can also turn the question that history generates around. The future of the US-China economic relationship is not just a question of whether the United States has the domestic politics to sustain its position as a debtor state, but whether China has the domestic politics to sustain its position as a large-scale creditor state lending in another state's currency. Whether the Chinese leadership can make a decisive strategic shift away from the economic relationship with the United States in its present form may turn on how quickly it can create a more consumer-oriented economic culture so that domestic demand could be radically expanded. The domestic politics of both sides of the economic relationship between the United States and China now compound all the difficulties that were created by interdependence and the way it developed.

## The state, politics and the financial crisis

By early 2009, the future of the economic relationship between the United States and east Asia, and China in particular, had come to turn on a set of fundamentally political questions that the problems of interdependence and the way it has been managed by governments have created. There is no economic resolution to China's dilemma about what to do about its dollar holdings. There is only a political judgement to be made in Beijing about how to deal with the risks that China is running, and not an objective economic fix to be hit upon. The Chinese leadership must decide when the Chinese economy can absorb the short- and medium-term cost of reducing the state's dollar portfolios to contain the long-term losses that its past decision-making have ensured are one day inevitable. Within the Chinese leadership, what to do, and when to do it, will be contested because the political fallout from the economic tumult that a radical shift in exchange rate policy will bring about is likely to be severe because of its consequences for employment. Meanwhile, in the United States there will eventually have to be a political debate about what to do about Fannie Mae and Freddie Mac and whether it is either desirable or sustainable for the American state to have responsibility for these two corporations. Whilst the resolution of that question matters a great deal economically for the future of the financial relationship between the United States and east Asia, that debate is as likely to be as much about the politics of home ownership as the fiscal cost to the American state of maintaining the conservatorship and guarantees to the corporations' east Asian creditors.

Yet there will also be nothing new in politics proving crucial to how the economic relationship between the United States and east Asia plays out, or its accompanying impact on the entire international economy. The political nature of the general financial crisis and its fallout has frequently been lost in much commentary and analysis. Much of the early political narrative around the financial crisis centred on the behaviour of financial markets and the greed of the financial sector. Many assumed that the fundamental causes of the crisis lay in the primacy of markets over the state and politics, and that the state has now had to take responsibility for significant parts of financial sectors precisely because it was previously largely absent from any part of their operation. Although many financial corporations did behave in grossly reckless ways, the origins of the financial crisis in the Pacific economic relationship, and what that made possible, are also far more complex than this particular narrative suggested. Put simply, they were in significant part political and they involved the state in different ways. As Herman Schwartz and Leonard Seabrooke's recently edited volume on the subject shows, the politics of housing and housing finance are crucial to understanding the present nature of the international economy.[23]

The sub-prime mortgage boom that lay at the centre of the crisis was as much the product of the drive by successive American Presidents and the Congress to expand home ownership as it was new financial derivatives devised on Wall Street. American politicians wanted more home ownership and by definition that meant that they wanted banks and other financial corporations to lend to people who previously had not been given mortgages. Since the question of whether these new customers were creditworthy was not easily separated from the fact that a disproportionately low number of African-Americans and Hispanics were home owners in the United States, and since increasing lending to these groups was a policy goal of two administrations, sub-prime lending was politically protected. Meanwhile, the sub-prime boom and the accompanying financial bubble in mortgage-backed securities was made possible because the east Asian governments, and China's in particular, politically decided to arm themselves against currency speculators and also to stop short-term financial flows that if unchecked would have driven their exchange rates upwards against the dollar. The first decision came out of the east Asian government's understanding of the political consequences of the Asian financial crisis as well as the economic. Capital flight had devastated much of the region economically, but so politically had exposure to the power of the United States through the conditionality on which the IMF had insisted. Moreover, in deciding to continue to accumulate reserves to protect a competitive exchange rate, the Chinese leadership was pursuing a development strategy that it saw as crucial to maintaining political order.

In understanding the role of politics, the place of the state is crucial. On both sides of the economic relationship between the United States and east Asia, politics mattered in part because of the power of the state and what that power made possible. This is clearest on the east Asian side because there governments so overtly set out to use the power of state, via the accumulation of reserves and in China's case the deployment of capital controls, to create outcomes contrary to the ones that the financial and foreign exchange markets would have produced. In doing so these states established the pool of capital that made cheap borrowing possible for the American government, Fannie Mae and Freddie Mac, and, indirectly, corporations across the housing sector.

Nonetheless, the power of the state was important on the American side too. Certainly the American state's reach in economic matters is fragmented and in some respects weak and, as Lawrence Jacobs and Desmond King have recently said, in the context of the financial crisis, 'institutionally incoherent'.[24] The Securities and Exchange Commission acquiesced easily to the pressure of the investment banks in 2004 to reduce the restrictions on their borrowing and the consequences of that decision went well beyond those corporations for whom the Commission was responsible. From the moment the first phase of the financial crisis began in the summer of 2007 through to fallout of the Lehman bankruptcy, the American Treasury had to rely on trying to co-ordinate other agencies and cajoling financial corporations into certain lines of action to do much. When, then, the whole financial sector was in danger of meltdown in the autumn of 2008, the American executive had to negotiate and compromise with Congress to get effective emergency powers for the Treasury to act in any way likely to avert disaster. However, as Kevin Gotham has argued, the American state had been a crucial player via federal legislation and the activities of regulatory agencies in the moves that integrated local housing markets into international financial flows in the first place.[25]

More particularly, Fannie Mae and Freddie Mac's borrowing only happened because of the implicit political commitment that the American state could, and would, guarantee the debt that the two corporations issued and the confidence that gave investors, especially foreign central banks, to lend. That commitment existed because the American state had long been deeply involved in the American mortgage market. Over seven decades it had created incentives for financial corporations to involve themselves in primary mortgage lending or the secondary mortgage market, and it had provided an effective guarantee to a considerable amount of financial activity around home ownership. The legacy of the state's historical intervention mattered for the way the Clinton and Bush jnr administrations and Congress dealt with the issues around Fannie Mae and Freddie Mac. It was the reason why much of the political debate about the corporations took the substantive shape it did, and it was a significant part of the explanation as to why those who privileged home ownership over financial risk politically won the regulatory battle that took place in the middle of the decade even when, given the absence of accurate financial reporting from the two corporations, those risks were enormous.

However, the existence of state-capability itself is not a sufficient explanation of the crisis around Fannie Mae and Freddie Mac. Politics also mattered because of what those with state power chose politically to do, or not do, with that power. The politics of the two corporations' part in the mortgage boom was not pre-determined just because of the length, depth and historical difficulties of the American state's involvement in home ownership. The American state did carry the weight of the discriminatory politics of the past, but that mattered because many members of Congress, and Democrats in particular, chose to privilege remedying the consequences of that over dispassionate analysis of the financial facts in their decision-making. The regulatory rules over Fannie Mae and Freddie Mac that were in place between the beginning of the housing boom and the summer of 2008, and which left the two corporations free to drive the final part of the sub-prime expansion, were the product of a political contest between competing sets of politicians, the two corporations themselves, and interest groups, in which the different actors wished to use the power of the state for very different reasons. One political position won and the other lost. But if the Bush administration had been able to create and maintain an across-the-board Republican party position on the issue in 2003 through 2004 and procured some modest Democrat support in the Senate, the corporations would have been placed under a tougher regulatory regime that would have restricted their borrowing and investment portfolios. Under this scenario, they would have not been able to operate as they did from the latter part of 2004 and the sub-prime boom would almost certainly have ended earlier and with less disastrous fallout for the world economy. In understanding why that counter-factual did not happen, we need to turn to the specific conditions of American domestic politics. That the Bush administration and the Republican reformers in Congress failed in their aims and were unable to check Fannie Mae and Freddie Mac was in significant part the consequence of the political fact that because of the structure of campaign finance and lobbying in the United States, the two corporations were able to direct political services to individual members of Congress. Just as significantly, other issues of financial regulation were also politically contested in the years leading up to the boom. On the regulation of derivatives, there was a battle within Congress, and then between the Treasury and the Federal Reserve Board on one side and the Commodity Futures Trading Commission on the other. Whilst there was rather less political support for regulating derivatives than there was for creating new rules for Fannie Mae and Freddie Mac, the absence of regulation was nonetheless a judgement made by those who dominated the institutional decision-making process at the expense of those who would have decided differently.

In explaining these political outcomes, we also have to go beyond considering which material interests were practically served by the various political decisions that were made by American policy-makers and look at the way the issues at stake were politically constructed by different participants in the debates. Many American politicians were unwilling to confront the questions of financial risk around Fannie Mae and Freddie Mac because there was a high political price to accepting a narrative that might appear to question the sanctity of increasing the rate of home ownership among African-Americans and Hispanics. For many Democrats in Congress, the discourse of financial risk conceded too much general ground to their Republican opponents about the difficulties of changing the balance of opportunities for different social groups in such a conspicuously divided and unequal society. The consequence of the way in which home ownership had become framed as a policy issue in the United States was that the opponents of reform acted as if they were in denial about what was happening at Fannie Mae and Freddie Mac: since the problem was too politically awkward, therefore the problem could not exist. Interestingly, this mirrored the unwillingness of those acting in the financial markets to face up to the inherent risk of securitised sub-prime lending, in their case because there was short-term money to be made in not doing so. In this sense, the dominant political perspective in the United States on the financial risk inherent to the sub-prime boom, and its accompanying financial derivatives, was rather similar to the one that prevailed in the financial markets.

The actions of states also impact on economic interdependence through their international consequences. The way states politically deal with the opportunities and constraints of interdependence engenders further opportunities and constraints for other states. The growth strategy that the east Asian governments decided upon created the economic opportunity for the American sub-prime boom and the scale of Fannie Mae and Freddie Mac's expansion and borrowing. The borrowing of the American government and its willingness to allow a burgeoning current account deficit provided an outlet for east Asia's savings and made it possible for the east Asian governments to manage their exchange rates to support export-led growth.

The constraints created by other states for the east Asian states were overt. The first rationale for the strategy of accumulating dollar reserves was a political response to those that had played out through the Asian financial crisis. The east Asian governments had to make choices about economic matters in the context of an international economy that they had not politically shaped and in which the United States could, through the IMF, make demands about the organisation of their economies and decision-making. Over time, for the Chinese leadership in particular, the external politics of the economic relationship with the United States created an ever-deeper constraint on its prudent policy options. From the start, it was left with no purchase on whether the American government acted, or not, to maintain the value of China's dollar lending and investments, when that question was of immense significance for China's future. Thereafter, unless and until it was willing to reverse its economic strategy, the Chinese leadership had no choice but to keep leaving itself ever further at the mercy of decisions made in Washington. As a result, any eventual reversal of policy will be that much more domestically costly for China. For the United States, the constraints generated by the Chinese state were certainly less immediately problematic. Nonetheless, American politicians and the Federal Reserve Board did have reason to fear that decisions made in Beijing could precipitate a large-scale crisis of foreign confidence in the dollar. Consequently, even on the American side there was at times some degree of external state constraint on what those responsible for economic policy could judiciously decide to do. The dollar weakness that was the central tension of the Pacific economic relationship after 2002 helped create the context in which the Federal Reserve tightened monetary policy from 2004 and the mortgage boom began to unravel. Most conspicuously, the American government was constrained by what the Chinese and Japanese governments could accept in how it could deal with the Fannie Mae and Freddie Mac crisis. Today, unsurprisingly, the constraints generated by other states on how governments can deal with the fallout of the financial crisis remain tighter on the east Asian side than the American. China is not only at risk to a policy move in Washington that precipitates a large fall in the dollar to an unprecedented degree, but the leadership would now have to deal with such a crisis during, or after, a period of significantly reduced growth. By contrast, the United States enjoyed huge monetary and fiscal discretion in the autumn of 2008 and continued to do so over the following months. The problems the Chinese government faces because of interdependence have thus far not proved a constraint on the Federal Reserve Board printing money or the American government hugely increasing its borrowing.

Yet even on the American side of the relationship, the Chinese government's domestic political response to the contingencies produced by American domestic politics could well become increasingly problematic looking to the future. In taking on the liabilities of Fannie Mae and Freddie Mac, the American state has become far more constrained by its internal politics around home ownership in how it can react to any eventual external imperative for retrenchment than it has hitherto. This is in part a practical question in that withdrawing the state's support for this part of the mortgage sector would at any time be very likely to have deleterious market consequences. But it is also a matter of political expectations. When a state once takes responsibility in an area, it creates a presumption among its citizens that the politicians in office will use the power of the state to respond to moments of difficulty in that sphere, and any government usually cannot ignore those expectations without fighting a political battle to repudiate them. Meanwhile, the Chinese leadership has already become constrained by the domestic anger felt about the financial relationship with the United States, and would face a huge problem if the interests and passions at stake in American domestic politics produced a situation that created even the suggestion that the American government could renege on its commitment to honour Fannie Mae and Freddie Mac's debt. Even without such a scenario, the domestic anger in China is likely to rise further if and when the Chinese leadership accepts that it should begin to take the significant losses ahead and tries to retreat from its present commitment to the dollar. How the Chinese leadership manages this political problem will then become part of the external constraint that American policy-makers themselves will face in the future. American domestic politics and Chinese domestic politics will have serious consequences for the other state as will the way each government reacts to that problem.

Recognising the place of politics in the way the dynamics of interdependence have played out in the economic relationship between the United States and China has important implications for the way in which international political economy is conceived as an academic subject. Despite the original aspiration of the subject to analyse the interaction of the economic and the political, the language of 'globalisation', which became commonplace in much analysis within the field over the past two decades, in itself effectively negated politics because its central premise was that globalising economic forces were reconstituting the world and subjugating political choices to international economic realities. Whilst many scholars have recognised that states were not as impotent economically as this discourse suggested,[26] the actual contingencies of the particular domestic politics of individual states tended to be neglected in much of the literature beyond the recognition that more right-wing-oriented and more left-wing-oriented governments might wish to choose different macro-economic policies.[27]

Yet, as the development of American policy towards Fannie Mae and Freddie Mac shows, the political actions of policy-makers consistently shape and reshape the consequences of economic interdependence and they do so from matters that go far beyond macro-economic policy. Since they do, we need tools of analysis that the study of the international economy conceived as a discrete academic subject cannot generate. As Nicola Philipps has argued, since specific states with their distinct features are 'fundamentally constitutive' of the international economy, international political economy cannot separate itself as a field of enquiry from comparative politics and comparative political economy.[28] Whatever issues generated by the international economy we are analysing, we need to pay attention to political specifics and contingencies. In doing this, we need to avoid the trap of assuming that the economic is foundational and that the political is merely a response to the economic. Put simply, the political is part of the nature of economic interdependence itself.[29] We also need to recognise that since relations between states as separate political actors also shape the political nature of economic interdependence, international political economy should not be analytically separated from international relations. The political relations that have developed between the United States and China cannot possibly be the same as those between the United States and Japan, however much the Japanese and Chinese states operate under similar economic constraints in relation to the dollar and American monetary policy, or pursue much the same policy over foreign exchange reserves. Neither can these different political relations between different states not have an impact upon the way that the dilemmas generated by economic interdependence are conceived by those who have to make policy decisions in the face of them. Since these specific political relations between states are themselves part of the opportunities and constraints of economic interdependence, they need to be analysed as such.[30]

## The political limits of economic interdependence

The development of the financial crisis and its aftermath have made certain things clear about the consequences of economic interdependence that were less apparent in the experiences of states over the previous two decades. The 1990s and early years of the 21st century had appeared to suggest, first, that open international capital flows created potentially severe problems primarily for developing-country and emerging-market states, and, second, that economies where governments had adapted their economic policies to the opportunities that trade openness created were most likely to prosper. In the wake of the financial crisis, both of these judgements have proved at least partially misleading. The risk that access to cheap capital would produce reckless borrowing and deleterious consequences for an entire economy proved to apply to rich states, as well as to developing-country and emerging-market states. Although, unlike developing-country and emerging-market states in the 1990s, the United States had borrowed in its own currency and done so in significant part from other states with a policy incentive to lend, it eventually paid a high price for availing itself of the opportunity that international financial flows created. The risks of excessive international borrowing by corporations and households in a major economy went beyond exposure to the inherent volatility of financial markets. The financial flows involved deepened and reinforced the consequences of economic interdependence for all states because they tied so many markets, financial and otherwise, together. The securitisation of housing finance, and the way in which financial sectors around the world absorbed the products it generated, was at the centre of this problem. For developing-country governments themselves, the pattern of international financial flows since the beginning of the first phase of the financial crisis has only reinforced the conclusion that many of them had drawn during the 1990s that they simply cannot rely on integrated, supposedly free-flowing capital markets producing a steady supply of relatively cheap capital. Cross-border private financial flows started to fall sharply in the summer of 2007 and fell massively during the last quarter of 2008.[31] As the financial crisis entered its third phase, western investors returned to national markets, and once rich-state governments intervened to rescue financial sectors from collapse, banks in those countries were compelled into lending domestically rather than abroad.[32]

Openness to trade was shown to be at least in part a liability for states during a time of crisis in world demand. Export-led growth proved vulnerable to the fallout of trade interdependence. It left states too dependent on demand in markets in relation to which, by definition, they had no policy tools by which that demand could be resurrected. It also left them exposed to other states making protectionist moves to deal with the crisis. Especially in times of recession, economic interdependence creates severe domestic political problems for states, and, as argued in the introduction, governments will not necessarily respond to those difficulties by doing what is anything like most economically efficient. Even in rich states, economic nationalism is not a historical relic, and it will almost certainly never be because settling the terms of trade and financial flows with other states entails imposing at least short-term damage on the employment and income prospects of some groups of producers.

Meanwhile, the old and well-understood problems of economic interdependence endure. The financial crisis and its fallout have demonstrated once again that exchange rate management remains one of the most acute difficulties that economic interdependence creates for states. Despite their attempt to address this problem since the Asian financial crisis, the east Asian states have simply not been able to escape exchange rate problems. Ultimately, the efforts to create an east Asian dollar standard have failed. Before the first phase of the financial crisis began, some east Asian states had already abandoned their efforts to maintain currency stability. Between early 2002 and the middle of 2007, Indonesia, South Korea, Singapore Thailand, and the Philippines all saw large appreciations in their real exchange rate with the dollar.[33] Once the third-phase of the financial crisis began, various emerging-market states, including some in east Asia, faced full-scale currency crises with money exiting these economies at nearly the same speed and volume as it had during the Asian financial crisis. This fate befell states with current account surpluses as well as those with deficits. South Korea was hit particularly hard, despite having acted as systematically as any east Asian state to try to ensure that there could be no repetition of the earlier crisis and holding the sixth-largest portfolio of foreign exchange reserves of any state in the world. To try to abate the currency crisis it faced in the autumn of 2008, the South Korean government was forced to use the state's foreign exchange reserves to guarantee foreign currency debts and provide dollars to corporations.[34] Rather than finding any region-wide protection in the provisions of the Chiang Mai Initiative, the Bank of Korea ended up turning to the Federal Reserve Board to procure liquidity facilities and a $30 billion swap. When it mattered, the collective arrangements established by ASEAN Plus-Three to deal with a currency crisis of any of its member-states proved irrelevant.

Exchange rate problems in a world of economic interdependence endure because of the conjunction of the structural monetary and financial power enjoyed by the United States and the psychology of foreign exchange markets. Beyond the euro-zone, which may yet still be tested by the fallout of the financial crisis, states have not found a way around the dilemmas that these realities create for them. Whatever the long-term pressures on the dollar, the crisis of the autumn of 2008 vividly demonstrated that at times of panic and fear it remains the currency in which investors have most confidence. Despite all the question marks about the future of the financial relationship between the United States and east Asia raised by the events around Fannie Mae and Freddie Mac, the dollar strengthened significantly in the foreign exchange markets in the final quarter of 2008. Moreover, it did so as the American federal borrowing requirement was ballooning and the Federal Reserve Board was slashing interest rates. Meanwhile the states that were most afflicted by currency problems proved willing to turn back to the IMF, with an array of governments accepting loans in late 2008 and early 2009 from the international financial institution. Two of these states – Latvia and Hungary – were members of the European Union (EU) and the dominant member-states of the EU appeared more than willing to let the IMF, and with it the United States, deal with these states' currency and financial problems, despite the apparent opportunity that existed to tie them closer to the euro-zone. Providing emergency credit to new member-states proved a burden that the German government in particular did not want to carry. Certainly, recent developments have not simply strengthened American power. Since the onset of the third phase of the financial crisis both foreign central banks and private investors have drawn a very sharp line between the short term and the long term in their willingness to purchase dollar assets, and, despite the success of the Bush administration in procuring a measure of policy change in Beijing, President Obama has had to acquiesce to China's efforts to depreciate its currency. Nonetheless, the fallout of the financial crisis has demonstrated once again just how far American monetary and financial power and American macro-economic autonomy shape the international economic world in which other states have to operate.

For all the hopes invested in it by liberal optimists, economic interdependence itself cannot be a panacea to re-establish the conditions that produced rising prosperity and living standards across much of the world over the past two decades. The economic opportunities bestowed by interdependence have turned out to be more problematic than the optimists, and governments in those states that had in the past most benefitted from them, had supposed. Moreover, politics always complicates the opportunities that economic interdependence undoubtedly does create. Politics puts limits on what governments can readily choose to do in the economic policy decisions they have the autonomy to make, and the consequences of those limits then play their part in shaping and restricting the choices open to other governments. Interdependence is an economic and political problem that has to be permanently managed by governments. In today's world, the domestic and international political complexity of the economic relationship between the United States and China has become a major structural international economic problem. Having, directly and indirectly, driven so much of the economic growth across the world between 2002 and 2008 and created a particular set of interdependencies that played out through the financial crisis, this economic relationship in its present form would now appear to be quite probably politically unsustainable beyond the short term. The changes that dismantling, or adjusting that relationship will bring, will produce yet more economic turbulence of a kind that will hurt all states integrated into the international economy, and bequeath a whole new set of political problems of interdependence.

# Notes

## Chapter 1

1 See R. Boyer and T. Yamada, *Japanese Capitalism in Crisis* (London: Routledge, 2000); R. Henning, *Currencies and Politics in the United States, Germany and Japan* (Washington DC: Institute for International Economics, 1994).

2 A. Greenspan, *The Age of Turbulence: Adventures in a New World* (London: Allen Lane, 2007), pp. 159–160.

3 See I. Takatoshi, 'US Political Pressure and Economic Liberalisation in East Asia', in J. A. Frankel and M. Kahler (eds) *Regionalism and Rivalry: Japan and the United States in Asia-Pacific* (Chicago: Chicago University Press, 1994).

4 On the conditionality demanded by the IMF during the 1990s and the Asian financial crisis in particular see M. Feldstein, 'Refocusing the IMF', *Foreign Affairs*, 77 2 (1998) 20–33.

5 See N. Lardy, *Integrating China into the Global Economy* (Washington DC: Brookings Institution Press, 2002); S. Panitchpakdi, *China and the WTO: Changing China, Changing the World* (Singapore: Wiley and Sons, 2002).

6 For the argument that the euro was created as a response to the problems created by American power see C. R. Henning, 'Systemic Conflict and Regional Monetary Integration: the Case of Europe', *International Organisation*, 52 3 (1998) 537–573.

7 For a discussion of these issues see J. Kirshner, 'Dollar Primacy and American Power: What's at Stake', *Review of International Political Economy*, 15 3 (2008) 418–438; K. McNamara, 'A Rivalry in the Making: The Euro and International Monetary Power', *Review of International Political Economy*, 15 3 (2008) 439–459.

8 See N. Roubini and B. Setser, 'The Future of the International Monetary Fund', in R. Samans, M. Uzan and A. Lopez-Claros, *The International Monetary System: The IMF and the G20: A Great Transformation in the Making* (Basingstoke: Palgrave Macmillan, 2007).

9 On the international impact of China's economic rise, see D. Lampton, *The Three Faces of Chinese Power: Might, Money and Minds* (Los Angeles: University of California Press, 2008); S. Shirk, *China: Fragile Superpower* (Oxford: Oxford University Press, 2008).

10 R. I. McKinnon, *Exchange Rates Under the East Asian Dollar Standard: Living with Conflicted Virtue* (Cambridge, MA: MIT Press, 2005), p. 36

11 McKinnon, *Exchange Rates Under the East Asian Dollar Standard*, p. 5.

12 McKinnon, *Exchange Rates Under the East Asian Dollar Standard*, p. 6

13 L. Summers, 'The US Current Account Deficit and the Global Economy', Per Jacobsson Lecture Delivered in Washington DC, 3 October 2004, p. 8.

14 See in particular M. Dooley, D. Folkerts-Landau and P. Garber, *The Revived Bretton Woods System: The Effects of Periphery Intervention and Reserve Management on Interest Rates & Exchange Rates in Centre Countries*, NBER Working Paper No. 10332 (Cambridge MA: National Bureau of Economic Research, 2004); N. Ferguson and M. Schularick, 'Chimerica and the Global Asset Market Boom', *International Finance*, 10 3 (2007) 215–239; D. H. Levey and S. S. Brown, 'The Overstretch Myth', *Foreign Affairs*, 84 3 (2005) 1; D. H. Levey and S. S. Brown, 'Reply', *Foreign Affairs*, 84 4 (2005) 198–200.

15 L. Seabrooke, *The Social Sources of Financial Power: Domestic Legitimacy and International Financial Orders* (Ithaca: Cornell University Press, 2006), pp. 109–110.

16 See, for example, D. Held, A. McGrew, D. Goldblatt and J. Perraton, *Global Transformations: Politics, Economics and Culture* (Palo Alto CA: Stanford University Press, 1999).

17 S. Strange, *The Retreat of the State: The Diffusion of Power in the World Economy* (Cambridge: Cambridge University Press, 1996).

18 J. N. Rosenau, *Along the Domestic-Foreign Frontier: Exploring Governance in a Turbulent World* (Cambridge: Cambridge University Press, 1997).

19 A.-M. Slaughter, *A New World Order* (Princeton: Princeton University Press, 2004).

20 C. Hay, 'Introduction', in C. Hay (ed.), *New Directions in Political Science* (Basingstoke: Palgrave, 2010), p. 6.

21 P. Hirst, G. Thompson and S. Bromley, *Globalisation in Question*, 3rd edn (Cambridge: Polity Press, 2009); M. Moran, 'Policy-Making in an Interdependent World', in C. Hay (ed.) *New Directions in Political Science* (Basingstoke: Palgrave, 2010).

22 See H. Thompson, *Might, Right, Prosperity and Consent: Representative Democracy and the International Economy* (Manchester: Manchester University Press, 2008).

23 See M. D. Bordo, B. Eichengreen and D. A. Irwin, 'Is Globalisation Today Really Different than Globalization a Hundred Years Ago?', NBER Working Paper No. 7195 (Cambridge MA: National Bureau of Economic Research, 2004.

24 L. Weiss, *The Myth of the Powerless State: Governing the Economy in a Global Era* (Cambridge: Polity Press, 1998); L. Mosley, *Global Capital and National Governments* (Cambridge: Cambridge University Press, 2003).

25 G. Garrett, *Partisan Politics in the Global Economy* (Cambridge: Cambridge University Press, 1998); D. Rodrik, *One Economics, Many Recipes: Globalisation, Institutions and Economic Growth* (Princeton: Princeton University Press, 2007); P. A. Hall and D. Sosicke, *Varieties of Capitalism: The Institutional Foundations of Comparative Advantage* (Oxford: Oxford University Press, 2001).

26 E. Helleiner, *States and the Re-emergence of Global Finance* (Ithaca: Cornell University Press, 1996).

27 See, for example, D. Swank and S. Steimo, 'The New Political Economy of Taxation in Advanced Capitalist Democracies', *American Journal of*

*Political Science*, 46 3 (2002) 642–645; D. Swank, *Global Capital, Political Institutions and Policy Change in Developed Welfare States* (Cambridge: Cambridge University Press, 2002); C. Hay, 'Globalisation's Impact on States', in J. Ravenhill (ed.) *Global Political Economy*, 2nd edn (Oxford: Oxford University Press, 2008); D. Rodrik and E. Kaplan, 'Did the Malaysian Capital Controls Work?', in S. Edwards and J. Frankel (eds) *Preventing Currency Crises in Emerging Markets* (Chicago: University of Chicago Press, 2002).

28 See Thompson, *Might, Right, Prosperity and Consent.*

29 See C. Hay, *The Political Economy of New Labour: Labouring under False Pretences* (Manchester: Manchester University Press, 1999).

30 M. Weber, 'The Profession and Vocation of Politics', in P. Lassman and R. Speirs (eds) *Weber: Political Writings* (Cambridge: Cambridge University Press, 1994).

31 H. Thompson, 'The Modern State and its Adversaries', *Government and Opposition*, 41 1 (2006) 23–42.

32 See, for example, W. Reno, 'The Privatisation of Sovereignty and the Survival of Weak States', in B. Hibou (ed.) *Privatising the State* (London: Hurst Company and Publishers, 2004).

33 See, for example, R. O. Keohane and J. S. Nye, *Power and Interdependence: World Politics in Transition* (Boston MA: Little Brown, 1977); R. Keohane, *After Hegemony: Co-operation and Discord in the World Political Economy* (Princeton: Princeton University Press, 1984); G. J. Ikenberry, *Liberal Order and Imperial Ambition* (Cambridge: Polity, 2006); J. Nye, *The Paradox of American Power: Why the World's only Superpower Can't Go it Alone* (Oxford: Oxford University Press, 2002).

34 R. O. Keohane, 'Multilateralism: an Agenda for Research', *International Journal*, 45 (1990) 742.

35 G. J. Ikenberry, *Liberal Order and Imperial Ambition*, pp. 261–262.

36 Quoted in J. Frieden, *Global Capitalism: Its Rise and Fall in the Twentieth Century* (New York: W. W. Norton, 2006), p. 341.

37 C. Hay, 'Introduction', p. 6.

38 J. J. Mearsheimer, *The Tragedy of Great Power Politics* (London: W. W Norton and Company, 2001), p. 371.

39 E. H. Carr, *The Twenty Years' Crisis, 1919–1939: An Introduction to the Study of International Relations* (Basingstoke: Palgrave, 2001); K. Waltz, 'Globalisation and American Power', *The National Interest*, 59 (2000) 46–56.

40 See K. Waltz, 'The Myth of National Interdependence', in C. Kindleberger (ed.) *The International Corporation* (Cambridge MA: MIT Press, 1970); J. M. Grieco, 'Anarchy and the Limits of Cooperation: A Realist Critique of the Newest Liberal Institution', *International Organisation* 42 3 (1988) 485–507.

41 Mearsheimer, *The Tragedy of Great Power Politics*, p. 371; K. Waltz, 'Globalisation and American Power', *The National Interest*, 59 (2000) 46.

42 K. Waltz, 'Structural Realism After the Cold War', *International Security*, 25 1 (2000) 14.

43 Waltz, 'Globalisation and American Power', 56.
44 Mearsheimer, *The Tragedy of Great Power Politics*, p. 402
45 For an almost exclusively international explanation of the sub-prime and mortgage-back securities boom see M. Wolf, *Fixing Global Finance: How to Curb Financial Crises in the Twenty-First Century* (New Haven: Yale University Press, 2009). For an explanation of the sub-prime mortgage crisis centred on the psychology of irrational exuberance in financial markets see R. J. Shiller, *The Sub-Prime Solution: How Today's Global Financial Crisis Happened and What to Do About it* (Princeton: Princeton University Press, 2008).

## Chapter 2

1 See E. Prasad, R. Rajan, and A. Subramanian, 'Foreign Capital and Economic Growth', International Monetary Fund Research Department, August 2006. Available at http://www.imf.org/external/np/speeches/2006/082506.htm
R. Rajan, 'Global Imbalances: an Assessment', International Monetary Fund Research Department, October 2005. Available at http://www.imf.org/external/np/speeches/2005/102505.htm
2 B. Bernanke, 'The Global Saving Glut and the US Current Account Deficit', The Homer Jones Lecture Delivered in St. Louis, Missouri, 15 April 2005. Available at http://www.federalreserve.gov/boarddocs/speeches/2005/2005-0414/default.htm
3 K. J. Forbes, *Why Do Foreigners Invest in the United States?* National Bureau of Economic Research Working Paper No. 13908 (Cambridge MA: National Bureau of Economic Research, 2008).
4 R. Rajan, 'Perspectives on Global Imbalances', Remarks at the Global Financial Imbalances Conference in London, 23 January 2006. Available at http://www.imf.org/external/np/speeches/2006/012306.htm
5 Forbes, *Why Do Foreigners Invest in the United States?* See also P. O. Gourinchas and H. Rey, *International Financial Adjustment*, National Bureau of Economic Research Working Paper 11563 (Cambridge MA: National Bureau of Economic Research, 2005); M. Wolf, *Fixing Global Finance: How to Curb Financial Crises in the Twenty-First Century* (New Haven: Yale University Press, 2009).
6 See, for example, Bernanke, 'The Global Saving Glut'; L. Summers, 'Reflections on Global Account Imbalances and Emerging Markets Reserve Accumulation', L. K. Jha Memorial Lecture at the Reserve Bank of India, Mumbai, 24 March 2006.
7 See, for example, B. Setser and N. Roubini, 'How Scary is the Deficit?', *Foreign Affairs*, 84 4 (2005); Yu Yongding, 'Global Imbalances: China's Perspective', paper prepared for an International Conference on Global Imbalances at the International Institute of Economics Washington DC, 8 February 2007. Available at http://www.iie.com/publications/pb/pb07-4/yu.pdf

8 Bernanke, 'The Global Saving Glut'.
9 Wolf, *Fixing Global Finance,* pp. 98–110.
10 International Monetary Fund, World Economic Outlook Database, April 2007.
11 Wolf, *Fixing Global Finance,* p. 108.
12 See M. Zandi, *Financial Shock: Global Panic and Government Bailouts – How We Got Here and What Must be Done to Fix it,* updated edn (Upper Saddle River, NJ: FT Press 2009), pp. 67–80.
13 A. Greenspan, *The Age of Turbulence: Adventures in a New World* (London: Allen Lane, 2007), p. 233.
14 International Monetary Fund, World Economic Outlook Database, October 2008.
15 Quoted in D. Hale, 'Dodging the Bullet – This Time: the Asian Economic Crisis and US Economic Growth', *Brookings Review,* 16 3 (1998) 25.
16 T. J. Pempel, 'Restructuring Regional Ties', in A. Macintryre, T. J. Pempel and J. Ravenhill (eds) *Crisis as Catalyst: Asia's Dynamic Political Economy* (Ithaca: Cornell University Press, 2008), p. 167.
17 See R. Higgott, 'The Asian Economic Crisis: a Study in the Politics of Resentment', *New Political Economy,* 3 3 (1998) 333–356.
18 See S. N. Katada, 'From a Supporter to a Challenger: Japan's Currency Leadership in Dollar-Denominated East Asia', *Review of International Political Economy,* 15 3 (2008) 399–417.
19 See Y. C. Park and Y. Wang, 'The Chiang Mai Initiative and Beyond', *The World Economy,* 28 1 (2005) 91–101; R. C. Henning, *East Asian Financial Co-operation* (Washington DC: Institute for International Economics, 2002), ch. 3; J. Amyx 'Regional Financial Co-operation in East Asia Since the Asian Financial Crisis', in Macintryre, Pempel and Ravenhill (eds) *Crisis as Catalyst,* pp. 117–139.
20 The Joint Ministerial Statement of the 11th ASEAN+3 Finance Ministers' Meeting Held in Madrid, 4 May 2008, published by the Japanese Ministry of Finance. Available at http://www.mof.go.jp/english/if/as3_080504.pdf.
21 For scepticism about the capacity of the east Asian states to organise regionally to resist American monetary power see P. Bowles, 'Asia's Post-Crisis Regionalism: Bringing the State Back in, Keeping the United States out', *Review of International Political Economy,* 9 2 (2002) 244–270; N. Hamilton-Hart, 'Asia's New Regionalism: Government Capacity and Co-Operation in the Western Pacific', *Review of International Political Economy,* 10 2 (2003) 222–245.
22 Bowles, 'Asia's Post-Crisis Regionalism'.
23 Wolf, *Fixing Global Finance,* p. 39
24 International Monetary Fund, World Economic Outlook Database, October 2008.
25 Wolf, *Fixing Global Finance* p. 92.
26 See P. Bowles and B. Wang, 'Flowers and Criticism: The Political Economy of the Renminbi Debate', *Review of International Political Economy,* 13 2 (2006) 242–243.

27 See N. Lardy, *China's Unfinished Revolution* (Washington DC: Brookings Institution, 1998).
28 See E. Steinfeld, 'The Capitalist Embrace: China Ten years After the Asian Financial Crisis', in Macintryre, Pempel and Ravenhill (eds) *Crisis as Catalyst*, pp. 183–205.
29 Steinfeld, 'The Capitalist Embrace', p. 192.
30 D. Glickman, Statement by US Secretary of Agriculture at 2000 Commodity Classic in Orlando, 6 March 2000. Available at http://www.usda.gov/news/releases/2000/03/0072
31 See S. Wang, 'The Social and Political Implications of China's WTO Membership', *Journal of Contemporary China*, 9 25 (2000) 373–405; N. Lardy, *Integrating China into the Global Economy* (Washington DC: Brookings Institution, 2002).
32 P. Bowles and B. Wang, 'The Rocky Road Ahead: China, the US and the Future of the Dollar', *Review of International Political Economy*, 15 3 (2008) 342–343.
33 B. Emmott, *Rivals: How the Power Struggle between China, India and Japan will Shape our Next Decade* (London: Harcourt, 2008), p. 61.
34 International Monetary Fund, World Economic Outlook, April 2007, p. 22.
35 United States Department of the Treasury, Report on Foreign Portfolio Holdings of US Securities as of 30 June 2007, Historical Data. Available at http://www.treas.gov/tic/shlhistdat.html
36 In 2003, China's exports grew by 34.6 per cent and its imports by 37.1 per cent. In 2004, China's exports grew by 36 per cent and imports by 35.7 per cent. But, in 2005, China's exports grew by 28.4 per cent and its imports by 17.6 per cent. The US-China Business Council, 'Forecast 2008: China's Economy', p. 2. Available at http://www.uschina.org/public/documents/2008/02/2008-china-economy.pdf
37 Quoted in Bowles and Wang, 'Flowers and Criticism', 246. For a forthright nationalist attack on international attempts to force a revaluation on China starting from the argument that succumbing to such pressure in the second half of the 1980s had disastrous consequences for Japan see Anon, 'Who is Boosting a Revaluation of RMB?', *People's Daily*, 23 July 2003, English Internet edition. Available at http://english.peopledaily.com.cn/200307/23/eng20030723_120865.shtml
38 International Monetary Fund, World Economic Outlook Database, October 2008.
39 B. Clinton, *My Life* (New York: Knopf Publishing Group, 2004), p. 459.
40 Board of Governors of the Federal Reserve System, Discount Rate Changes: Historical Dates of Changes and Rates. Available at http://research.stlouisfed.org/fred2/data/DISCOUNT.txt
41 International Monetary Fund, World Economic Outlook Database, October 2008.
42 OECD, Stat Extracts, Country Statistical Profiles: The United States.
43 Wolf, *Fixing Global Finance*, p. 107.
44 Federal Reserve Board, Flow of Funds Accounts of the US Annual Flows and Outstanding 2005–2007 and Flow of Funds Accounts of the US Annual

Flows and Outstanding 1995–2004, December 2008. Available at http://www.federalreserve.gov/releases/z1/Current/annuals/a2005-2007.pdf; http://www.federalreserve.gov/releases/z1/Current/annuals/ a1995-2004.pdf

45 Federal Reserve Board, Flow of Funds Accounts of the US Annual Flows and Outstanding 2005–2007 and Flow of Funds Accounts of the US Annual Flows and Outstanding 1995–2004.

46 Agency debt is issued by various federal agencies, the Federal Home Loan Banks and Fannie Mae and Freddie Mac. Fannie Mae and Freddie Mac's bonds and securities constitute the largest component of agency debt.

47 The Chinese central bank has used private investors to make large-scale purchases of various dollar assets on its behalf. Consequently, the data published by the United States Treasury substantially under-records China's dollar holdings. B. Setser and A. Pandey, 'China's $1.7 Trillion Bet: China's External Portfolio and Dollar Reserves', Council on Foreign Relations Working Paper, January 2009, p. 10.

48 United States Department of the Treasury, Report on Foreign Portfolio Holdings of US Securities as of 30 June 2007, Historical Data, April 2008. Available at http://www.treas.gov/tic/shlhistdat.html

49 United States Department of the Treasury, Report on Foreign Portfolio Holdings of US Securities as of 30 June 2007, p. 16.

50 United States Department of the Treasury, Report on Foreign Portfolio Holdings of US Securities as of 30 June 2007, p. 24.

51 See Ferguson and Schularick, 'Chimerica and the Global Asset Market Boom'; R. Cooper, *Policy Briefs in International Economics*: *Living with Global Imbalances: A Contrarian View* (Washington DC: Institute for International Economics, 2005); D. H. Levey and S. S. Brown, 'The Overstretch Myth', *Foreign Affairs*, 84 3 (2005); R. Clarida, 'Japan, China and the US Current Account Deficit', *CATO Journal*, 25 1 (2005) 111–114; R. J. Caballero, E. Farhi and P. O. Gourinchas, *An Equilibrium Model of 'Global Imbalances' and Low Interest Rates*, National Bureau of Economic Research Working Paper No. 11996 (Cambridge MA: National Bureau of Economic Research 2006).

52 M. P. Dooley, D. Folkerts-Landau, and P. M. Garber, *The Revived Bretton Woods System: The Effects of Periphery Intervention and Reserve Management on Interest Rates and Exchange Rates in Centre Countries*, National Bureau of Economic Research Working Paper No. 10332 (Cambridge MA: National Bureau of Economic Research, 2004); M. P. Dooley, D. Folkerts-Landau, and P. M. Garber, 'The US Current Account Deficit and Economic Development: Collateral for a Total Return Swap', National Bureau of Economic Research Working Paper No. 10727 (Cambridge MA: National Bureau of Economic Research, 2004).

53 On the benefits the United States secured from China's competitive exchange rate see D. D. Hale and L. Hughes Hales, 'Reconsidering Revaluation: The Wrong Approach to the US-Chinese Trade Imbalance', *Foreign Affairs*, 87 1 (2008).

54 Dooley, Folkerts-Landau and Garber, *The Revived Bretton Woods System*.

55 'Bank of Korea Backtracks on Forex Intervention', *Financial Times*, 19 May 2005; 'Korea to Limits its Dollar Holdings', *Washington Post*, 23 February 2005.

56 P. Volcker, 'An Economy on Thin Ice', *Washington Post,* 10 April 2005.
57 Setser and Roubini, 'How Scary is the Deficit?'.
58 B. Eichengreen, *Global Imbalances and the Lessons of Bretton Woods,* National Bureau of Economic Research Working Paper No. 10497 (Cambridge MA: National Bureau of Economic Research 2004). See also H. Thompson, 'Debt and Power: The United States' Debt in Historical Perspective', *International Relations,* 21 3 (2007) 304–323.
59 M. Goldstein and N. R. Lardy, *China's Role in the Revived Bretton Woods System: A Case of Mistaken Identity,* International Economics Institute working paper 05-2 (Washington DC: International Economics Institute, 2005), pp. 14 and 16. On the Japanese government's perspective on the difficulties of the relationship see R. Taggart Murphy, 'East Asia's Dollars', *New Left Review,* 40, July–August (2006) 39–64.
60 'Insight: Reserve Judgement on the Dollar', *Financial Times,* 23 September 2008.
61 See H. Paulson, 'A Strategic Economic Engagement: Strengthening US-China Ties', *Foreign Affairs,* 87 5 (2008).
62 See Bowles and Wang, 'The Rocky Road Ahead'.
63 Paulson, 'A Strategic Economic Engagement'.
64 Goldstein and Lardy, *China's Role in the Revived Bretton Woods System,* p. 7.
65 Quoted in H. F. Hung, 'Rise of China and the Global Overaccumulation Crisis', *Review of International Political Economy,* 15 2 (2008) 150.
66 On the strategic dilemmas China has faced over the past two decades and its response to them see A. Goldstein, *Rising to the Challenge: China's Grand Strategy and International Security* (Stanford: Stanford University Press, 2005).
67 United States Department of the Treasury, Report on Foreign Portfolio Holdings of US Securities as of 30 June 2007, Historical Data, April 2008.
68 Data provided by Brad Setser.
69 'Kuwait Drops Dollar Peg', *Kuwait Times,* 21 May 2007.
70 'Gulf States Consider Revaluing Currencies, Persons Familiar Says', *Bloomberg,* November 18, 2007.
71 United States Department of the Treasury, TIC Monthly Data Reports on Cross-Border Financial Flows for January 2005 and January 2008.

## Chapter 3

1 Other states do intervene in mortgage finance through institutional agencies. Canada has something similar to Federal Housing Administration mortgage insurance and Germany has a government-backed institution to support mortgage finance. Several Asian states – Japan, South Korea, Singapore, India, Hong Kong, Malaysia, Pakistan, Thailand, Sri Lanka – have government housing finance agencies that support home ownership in one way or another. However, institutionally, no other state is involved in the range of ways the American state has been and only the Singapore state

provides a level of financial support comparable to the United States. R. K. Green and S. M. Wachter, 'The American Mortgage in Historical and International Context', *Journal of Economic Perspectives*, 19 4 (2005) 102–105; M. Davies, J. Gyntelberg and E. Chan, 'Housing Finance Agencies in Asia', *Bank for International Settlements Papers* 241 (2007).

2 L. Seabroke, *The Social Sources of Financial Power: Domestic Legitimacy and International Financial Orders* (Cornell University Press: Ithaca, 1996), ch. 5.

3 M. A. Weiss, 'Marketing and Financing Home Ownership: Mortgage Lending and Public Policy in the United States, 1918–1989', in W. J. Hausman (ed.) *Business and Economic History*, series 2 vol. 18 (Wilmington, Del.: Business History Conference, 1989), p. 112.

4 Green and Wachter, 'The American Mortgage in Historical and International Context', 94.

5 B. Bernanke, 'Housing, Housing Finance and Monetary Policy', Speech at the Federal Reserve Bank of Kansas City's Economic Symposium, Jackson Hole, Wyoming, August 31 2007. Available at http://www.federalreserve.gov/newsevents/speech/bernanke20070831a.htm

6 Green and Wachter, 'The American Mortgage in Historical and International Context', 94.

7 The RFC required co-operation from the states and most did not have the legal authority to do what the RFC stipulated. Consequently, the RFC distributes rather less money than the Hoover administration envisaged. Kenneth Jackson, *Crabgrass Frontier: The Suburbanisation of the United States* (Oxford: Oxford University Press, 1985), pp. 194–195. See J. L. Butkiewicz, 'The Impact of a Lender of Last Resort During the Great Depression: The Case of the Reconstruction Finance Corporation', *Explorations in Economic History* 32 2 (1995) 197–216; J. S. Olson, *Saving Capitalism: The Reconstruction Finance Corporation and the New Deal, 1933–1940* (Princeton: Princeton University Press, 1988).

8 C. L. Harriss, *History and Policies of the Home Owners' Loan Corporation* (New York: National Bureau of Economic Research, 1951), p. 9.

9 Jackson, *Crabgrass Frontier*, p. 196.

10 Integrated Financial Engineering Inc, 'Evolution of the US Housing Finance System: A Historical Survey and Lessons for Emerging Mortgage Markets', Prepared for the United States Department of Housing and Urban Development, Office of Policy Development and Research, p. 6.

11 C. M. Haar, *Federal Credit and Private Housing: The Mass Financing Dilemma* (London: McGraw Hill, 1960) p. 171.

12 United States Census Bureau, Census of Housing: Historical Census of Housing Tables, Home Ownership. Available at http://www.census.gov/hhes/www/housing/census/historic/owner.html

13 Bernanke, 'Housing, Housing Finance and Monetary Policy'.

14 Fannie Mae, Charter. Available at http://www.law.cornell.edu/uscode/html/uscode12/usc_sec_12_00001716—000-.html

15 Fannie Mae, Charter.

16 See L. White, *The Savings and Loans Debacle: Public Policy Lessons for Bank and Thrift Regulation* (Oxford: Oxford University Press, 1990).

17 T. Curry and L. Shibut, 'The Cost of the Savings and Loans Crisis: Truth and Consequences', *Federal Deposit Insurance Corporation Banking Review*, December (2000); International Monetary Fund, World Economic Outlook Database, October 2008.
18 United States Commission on Civil Rights, 1961 United States Commission on Civil Rights Book 4: Housing, p. 16.
19 B. Bernanke, 'The Community Reinvestment Act: Its Evolution and New Challenges', Speech at the Community Affairs Research Conference in Washington DC, 30 March 2007. Available at http://www.federalreserve.gov/newsevents/speech/Bernanke20070330a.htm
20 M. I. Gelfand, *A Nation of Cities: The Federal Government and Urban America, 1933–1965* (Oxford: Oxford University Press), p. 123.
21 Quoted in Jackson, *Crabgrass Frontier*, p. 208.
22 Quoted in 1961 United States Commission on Civil Rights, p. 16. On redlining and its consequences see A. E. Hiller, 'Redlining and the Home Owners' Loan Corporation', *Journal of Urban History*, 29 4 (2003) 394–420; Jackson, *Crabgrass Frontier*, ch. 11; 1961 United States Commission on Civil Rights Report.
23 1961 United States Commission on Civil Rights Report, p. 17.
24 G. Lipsitz, 'The Possessive Investment in Whiteness: Racialised Social Democracy and the "White" Problem in American Studies', *American Quarterly* 47 3 (1995) 372.
25 1961 United States Commission on Civil Rights Report, pp. 25–31.
26 Haar, *Federal Credit and Private Housing*, p. 221.
27 United States Commission on Civil Rights; 1959 United States Commission on Civil Rights Report, p. 534.
28 1961 United States Commission on Civil Rights Report, pp. 140 and 145.
29 M. Carliner, 'Development of Federal Home Ownership Policy', *Housing Policy Debate*, 9 2 (1998) 311.
30 Seabrooke, *The Social Sources of Financial Power*, pp. 117–118.
31 United States Census Bureau, Housing Vacancies and Home Ownership, Historical Tables: Home Ownership Rates for the US and the Regions. Available at http://www.census.gov/hhes/www/housing/hvs/historic/index.html
32 G. Masnick, 'Home Ownership Trends and Racial Inequality in the US in the 20th Century', Working Paper W01-4, Joint Centre for Housing Studies, Harvard University, p. 7.
33 S. Chomsisengphet and A. Pennington-Cross, 'The Evolution of the Sub-Prime Mortgage Market', *Federal Reserve Bank of St Louis Review*, 88 1 (2006) 37.
34 On the integration of housing finance into the dynamics of international financial flows see S. Sassen, 'Mortgage Capital and its Particularities: A New Frontier for Global Finance', *Journal of International Affairs*, 62 1 (2008) 187–212.
35 Chomsisengphet and Pennington-Cross, 'The Evolution of the Sub-Prime Mortgage Market', 38.
36 United States Government Accounting Office, *Financial Derivatives: Actions Needed to Protect the Financial System* (Washington DC: United States Government Accounting Office, May 1994), p. 8.

37 'GAO Seeks Sweeping Rules for Derivatives', *New York Times*, 30 January 1999.

38 'Taking a Hard New Look at Greenspan Legacy', *New York Times*, 8 October, 2008; 'Brooksley Born "Vindicated" as Swap Rules Take Shape', *Bloomberg*, 13 November 2008; 'What Went Wrong', *Washington Post*, 15 October 2008.

39 Congress had enacted some smaller changes to the Act in 1989, 1992 and 1994.

40 'Agreement Reached on Overhaul of US Financial System', *New York Times*, 23 October 1999.

41 The Library of Congress, S. 2733. Federal Housing Enterprises Regulatory Reform Act of 1992; Available at http://thomas.loc.gov/cgi-bin/bdquery/z?d102:SN02733:@@@R

The Library of Congress, HR 6094, Federal Housing Enterprises Financial Safety and Soundness Act of 1992. Available at http://www.thomas.gov/cgi-bin/bdquery/z?d102:HR06094:@@@P

42 On the influence Fannie Mae and Freddie Mac had on the bill see J. Koppell, 'Hybrid Organisations and the Alignment of Interests: The Case of Fannie Mae and Freddie Mac', *Public Administration Review*, 61 4 (2001) 468–482.

43 R. Roberts, 'How Government Stoked the Mania', *Wall Street Journal*, 3 October 2008.

44 'How HUD Mortgage Policy Fed the Crisis', *Washington Post*, 10 June 2008.

45 United States Department of Housing and Urban Development: The Office of Policy Development and Research, 'Sub-Prime Lending, the Role of GSES and Risk-Based Pricing', March 2002, pp. 23–24.

46 United States Department of Housing and Urban Development, Press release, 'HUD Announces New Regulations to Provide $2.4 Trillion in Mortgages for Affordable Housing for 28.1 million Families', 3 November 2000. Available at http://www.ahfc.state.ak.us/iceimages/ news/110300-hud-announces-new-regulations.pdf

47 P. R. Argenti, 'Fannie Mae', Goldman Sachs and Executive Leadership Council and Foundation, p. 16. Available at http://mba.tuck.dartmouth.edu/pdf/2003-1-0070.pdf

48 'Fannie Mae Eases Credit to Aid Mortgage Lending', *New York Times*, 30 September 1999.

49 Argenti, 'Fannie Mae', p. 4.

50 'HUD says Mortgage Policies Hurt Blacks; Home Loans Giants Cited', *Washington Post*, 2 March 2000; 'Fannie Mae Chief Defends Record; HUD Chief Alleged Mortgage Giants' Policies Hurt Black Home Buyers', *Washington Post*, 3 March 2000.

51 Argenti, 'Fannie Mae', p. 12.

52 R. G. Bratt, 'Housing for Very Low-Income Households: The Record of President Clinton, 1993–2000', Working Paper W02-8, October 2002, Joint Centre for Housing Studies, Harvard University, p. 6.

53 A. B. Shlay, 'Low Income Home Ownership: American Dream or Delusion?', *Urban Studies*, 43 3 (2006) 516.

54 Bratt, 'Housing for Very Low-Income Households', p. 6.
55 'Deregulator Looks Back Unswayed', *New York Times*, 16 November 2008.

## Chapter 4

1 R. J. Schiller, *The Sub-Prime Solution: How Today's Financial Crisis Happened and What to Do About it* (Princeton: Princeton University Press, 2008), p. 32.
2 'In comes the waves', *The Economist*, 16 June 2005.
3 C. R. Morris, *The Trillion Dollar Meltdown: Easy Money, High Rollers, and the Great Credit Crash* (New York: Public Affairs, 2008), p. 66.
4 On the American housing boom see M. Zandi, *The Financial Shock: Global Panic and Government Bailouts – How We Got Here and What Must Be Done to Fix It*, updated edn (Upper Saddle River, NJ: FT Press, 2009); H. M. Schwartz, *Subprime Nation: American Economic Power, Global Capital Flows and Housing* (Ithaca: Cornell University Press, 2009); Schiller, *The Sub-Prime Solution*, chs. 2–4.
5 Joint Centre for Housing Studies of Harvard University, *The State of the Nation's Housing 2008* (Cambridge, MA: Joint Centre for Housing Studies of Harvard University, 2008), p. 29.
6 Securities Industry and Financial Markets Associations; Market Sector Statistics: Mortgage-Related Securities Issuance. Available at http://www.sifma.org/research/pdf/Mortgage_Related_Issuance.pdf
7 D. Di Martino and J. V. Duca, 'The Rise and Fall of Sub-Prime Mortgages', *Federal Reserve Bank of Dallas Economic Letter*, 2 11 (2007) 2.
8 United States House of Representatives, Transcript of Hearings Before the Committee on Oversight and Government Reform on the Credit Rating Agencies and the Financial Crisis, 22 October 2008, Chairman Waxon's Opening Statement. Available at http://oversight.house.gov/story.asp?ID=2255
9 United House of Representatives, Chairman Waxon's Opening Statement.
10 On the integration of the sub-prime market into Wall Street see R. Blackburn, 'The Subprime Crisis', *New Left Review*, 50 March–April (2008) 63–106.
11 Merrill Lynch, Annual Report 2008, p. 19. Available at http://ir.ml.com/sec.cfm?doctype=Annual
12 R. K. Green and S. M. Wachter, 'The American Mortgage in Historical and International Context', *Journal of Economic Perspectives*, 19 4 (2005) 99.
13 W. S. Frame and L. J. White, 'Fussing and Fuming over Fannie and Freddie: How Much Smoke, How Much Fire', *Journal of Economic Perspectives*, 19 2 (2005) 162.
14 'How HUD Mortgage Policy Fed the Crisis', *Washington Post*, 10 June 2008; R. S. England, 'The Rise of Private Label', *Mortgage Banking*, October (2006). Available at http://www.robertstoweengland.com/documents/MBM.10-06EnglandPrivateLabel.pdf

15 'White House Philosophy Stoked Mortgage Fire', *New York Times*, 20 December 2008.

16 United States Department of Housing and Urban Development, Press Release: 'The Daily Message', 25 June 2002. Available at http://www.hud.gov/news/focus.cfm?content=2002-06-25.cfm

17 United States Senate, S 811 (108th Congress), American Dream Downpayment Act. http://www.govtrack.us/congress/bill.xpd?bill=s108-811

18 Quoted in 'How Washington Failed to Rein In Fannie, Freddie', *Washington Post*, 14 September 2008.

19 Federal Reserve Board, Testimony of Chairman Alan Greenspan before the Senate Committee on Banking, Housing and Urban Affairs, 24 February 2004. Available at http://www.federalreserve.gov/boarddocs/testimony/2004/20040224/default.htm

20 Office of Federal Housing Enterprise Oversight, 'Report of the Special Examination of Freddie Mac, December 2003'.

21 'Fannie, Freddie Deflected Risk Warnings', *Washington Post*, 14 July 2008.

22 Office of Federal Housing Enterprise Oversight, 'Report of Findings to Date: Special Examination of Fannie Mae, 17 September 2004', p. i.

23 Office of Federal Housing Enterprise Oversight, 'OFHEO Report to Congress 2006', p. 17.

24 Office of Federal Housing Enterprise Oversight, 'OFHEO Report to Congress 2006', pp. 35–36.

25 Office of Federal Housing Enterprise Oversight, 'Report of the Special Examination of Fannie Mae, May 2006', p. 185.

26 Office of Federal Housing Enterprise Oversight, 'OFHEO Report to Congress 2006', pp. 6–7.

27 United States House of Representatives, Transcript of Hearing Before the House Financial Services Committee on HR 2575, The Secondary Mortgage Market Enterprises Regulatory Improvement Act, 25 September 2003, p. 65. Available at: http://commdocs.house.gov/committees/bank/hba92628.000/hba92628_0f.htm

28 United States House of Representatives, Transcript of Hearing Before the Sub-committee on Capital Markets of the House Financial Services Committee on the OFHEO Report: Allegations of Accounting and Management Failure at Fannie Mae, 6 October 2004, pp. 103–104. Available at http://commdocs.house.gov/committees/bank/hba97754.000/hba97754_0f.htm

29 United States House of Representatives, Transcript of Hearing, 6 October 2004, p. 15.

30 United States House of Representatives, Transcript of Hearing, 6 October 2004, p. 210.

31 United States House of Representatives, Transcript of Hearing before the House Committee on Financial Services, Testimony of John W. Snow, Secretary of the Treasury, 10 September 2003. Available at http://financialservices.house.gov/media/pdf/091003js.pdf

32 United States House of Representatives, HR 2803 (108th Congress) Housing Finance Regulatory Restructuring Act of 2003. Available at http://www.govtrack.us/congress/bill.xpd?bill=h108-2803 &tab=summary

33 S. W. Frame and L. J. Wright, 'Regulating Housing GSEs: Thoughts on Institutional Structure and Authorities', *Federal Reserve Bank of Atlanta: Economic Review*, second quarter (2004) footnote 17.
34 'Senate Banking Committee to Take Another Shot at GSE Reform', *Mortgage Banking*, 1 March 2006. Available at http://www.accessmylibrary.com/coms2/summary_0286-16016329_ITM
35 'Running a Covert Campaign Targeting GOP Senators', *Associated Press*, 19 October 2008.
36 John McCain, Remarks to the United States Senate on the Federal Housing Enterprise Regulatory Act Reform Act of 2005, 25 May 2006. Available at http://www.govtrack.us/congress/record.xpd?id=109-s20060525-16#sMonofilemx003Ammx002Fmmx002Fmmx002Fmhom
37 Govtrack.us, Vote on Passage of HR 1461 (109th Congress), Federal Housing Finance Reform Act of 2005. Available at http://www.govtrack.us/congress/vote.xpd?vote=h2005-547
38 L. Lerer, 'Fannie, Freddie Spent $200 m to Buy Influence', *Politico*, 16 July 2008. http://www.politico.com/news/stories/0708/11781.html
39 B. McClain, 'The Fall of Fannie Mae', *Fortune*, 24 January 2005; 'Fannie Mae Liberals', *Wall Street Journal*, 14 October 2004.
40 'Freddie Settles Investor Lawsuits', *Washington Post*, 21 April 2006.
41 United States House of Representatives, Transcript of Hearing, 6 October 2004, p. 118.
42 Quoted in 'Fannie, Freddie Deflected Warnings', *Washington Post*, 14 July 2008.
43 Quoted in B. McClain, 'The Fall of Fannie Mae', *Fortune*, 24 January 2005.
44 'Pressured to Take More Risk, Fannie Pushed to Breaking Point', *New York Times*, 4 October 2008.
45 United States House of Representatives, Transcript of Hearing, 25 September 2003, pp. 5 and 110.
46 United States House of Representatives, Transcript of Hearing Before the House Financial Services Committee on The Treasury Department's Views on the Regulation of the Government-Sponsored Enterprises, 10 September 2003, p. 5. Available at http://commdocs.house.gov/committees/bank/hba92231.000/hba92231_0f.htm
47 United States House of Representatives, Transcript of Hearing, 25 September 2003, p. 14.
48 United States House of Representatives, Transcript of Hearing, 25 September 2003, p. 157.
49 'HUD Sets New Policies, New Goals for Fannie, Freddie', *Washington Post*, 2 November 2004.
50 R. S. England, 'The Rise of Private Label'.
51 'Pressured to Take More Risks', *New York Times*.
52 P. J. Wallison and C. W. Calom, 'The Last Trillion-Dollar Commitment: The Destruction of Fannie Mae and Freddie Mac', American Enterprise Institute for Public Policy Research, September 2008; United States House of Representatives, Statement of James B. Lockhart III, Director, Federal Housing Finance Agency before the House Committee on

Financial Services on the Appointment of FHFA as Conservator for Fannie Mae and Freddie Mac, 25 September 2008.

53 United States House of Representatives, Statement of James B. Lockhart III, 25 September 2008. Available at http://www.house.gov/apps/list/hearing/financialsvcs_dem/lockhart092508.pdf

54 United States House of Representatives, Freddie Mac Internal E-Mails Released by the Committee on Oversight and Government Reform for Hearing on the Role of Fannie Mae and Freddie Mac in the Financial Crisis, 9 December 2008. http://oversight.house.gov/story.asp?ID=2252

55 United States House of Representatives, Hearing of the Committee on Oversight and Government Reform on the Role of Fannie Mae and Freddie Mac in the Financial Crisis, 9 December 2008, Chair's Opening Statement.

56 United States House of Representatives, Hearing of the Committee on Oversight and Government Reform on the Role of Fannie Mae and Freddie Mac in the Financial Crisis, 9 December 2008, Statement of Charles W. Calomiris, p. 8.

57 Frame and White, 'Fussing and Fuming over Fannie and Freddie', 175.

58 John Snow, Remarks to America's Community Bankers Association Government Affairs Conference, 9 March 2004. Available at http://www.treasury.gov/press/releases/js1225.htm

59 United States House of Representatives, Transcript of Hearing, 10 September 2003, p. 4.

60 'End of Illusions', *The Economist*, 17 July 2008.

## Chapter 5

1 B. S. Bernanke, 'Sub-Prime Mortgage Lending and Mitigating Foreclosures', Testimony Before the United States House of Representatives Committee on Financial Services, 20 September 2007. http://www.federalreserve.gov/newsevents/testimony/bernanke20070920a.htm

2 Office of Federal Housing Enterprise Oversight, 'OFHEO report to Congress 2008', pp. 3–4.

3 On the Bush administration and the Federal Reserve Board's response to the crisis in the second half of 2007 and early 2008 see M. Zandi, *Financial Shock: Global Panic and Government Bailouts – How We Got Here and What Must be Done to Fix It*, revised edn (Upper Saddle River, NJ: FT Press, 2009), pp. 193–209.

4 C. M. Rheinart and K. Rogoff, 'Is the 2007 US Sub-Prime Financial Crisis So Different? An International Historical Comparison', *American Economic Review: Papers and Proceedings*, 98 2 (2008) 340.

5 'How the Thundering Herd Faltered and Fell', *New York Times*, 9 November 2008.

6 On the meltdown in the market for sub-prime mortgage-backed securities and its fallout see Zandi, *Financial Shock*, p. 11.

7 'Asset-Backed Insecurity', *The Economist*, 17 January 2008; B. Setser, 'Sovereign Wealth and Sovereign Power: The Strategic Consequences of American Indebtedness', Council on Foreign Relations, Council Special Report No. 37, September 2008, p. 13.
8 'Unhappy New Year', *The Economist*, 21 December 2007; Setser, 'Sovereign Wealth and Sovereign Power', p. 14.
9 United States Treasury, Treasury International Capital System, 'TIC Monthly Report on Cross-Boarder Financial Flows for October 2007'.
10 X. Mei, 'It's US Dollar, not Yuan, that's the Global Problem', *The Shanghai Daily*, 21 April 2008.
11 United States Treasury, Treasury International Capital System, 'TIC Monthly Report on Cross-Border Financial Flows for August 2007'.
12 Office of Federal Housing Enterprise Oversight, 'OFHEO report to Congress 2008', p. 11.
13 United States House of Representatives, HR 1427 [$110^{th}$ Congress], Federal Housing Finance Reform Act of 2007. http://www.govtrack.us/congress/bill.xpd?bill=h110-1427
14 United States House of Representatives, Transcript of Hearing Before the Committee on Financial Services on Legislative Proposals on Government-Sponsored Enterprises Reform, 15 March 2007, p. 6. Available at http://frwebgate.access.gpo.gov/cgibin/getdoc.cgi?dbname =110_house_hearings &docid=f:35407.pdf
15 'House Tightens Reins on Fannie, Freddie', *Washington Post*, 23 May 2007.
16 'Russia Cuts Expose to US Mortgage Lenders', *Reuters*, 28 July 2008.
17 'Dollar Rises as Bernanke Says Fed May Extend Lending', *Bloomberg*, 8 July 2008
18 'Too Political to Fail', *Wall Street Journal*, 21 April 2008.
19 'Asian Stocks Drop, Led by Banks, as Credit Concerns Increase', *Bloomberg*, 15 July 2008.
20 'Bank of China Pots Slowest Profit Growth for Two Years', *Bloomberg*, 29 October 2008.
21 'Bank of China Flees Fannie-Freddie', *Financial Times*, 28 August 2008.
22 'Construction Bank Profit Rises 12% on Interest Income', *Bloomberg*, 24 October 2008.
23 'Asian Finance Stock Rise on Fannie, Freddie Takeover', *Bloomberg*, 8 September 2008.
24 W. Pesek, 'Fannie, Freddie Troubles Are Ominous for Asia', *Bloomberg*, 16 July 2008.
25 Statement of J. B. Lockhart III, Director, Federal Housing Finance Agency before the House Committee on Financial Services on the Appointment of FHFA as Conservator for Fannie Mae and Freddie Mac, September 25 2008. http://www.house.gov/apps/list/hearing/financialsvcs_dem/lockhart092508.pdf
26 'Paulson Risks Goldman Standard as Fannie, Freddie Shares Erode', *Bloomberg*, 21 August 2008.
27 'End of Illusions', *The Economist*, 17 July 2008.

28 'Fannie, Freddie Fall as Bank of China Reduces its Debt Holdings', *Bloomberg*, 29 August 2008.
29 Federal Reserve Board, Factors Affecting Reserve Balances, data for 17 July to 4 September 2008.
30 'Fannie and Freddie Doubts Grow', *Financial Times*, 29 August 2008; 'Fannie, Freddie Fall as Bank of China Reduces its Debt Holdings', *Bloomberg*, 29 August 2008.
31 'Fannie, Freddie Failure Could be World "Catastrophe" Yu Says', *Bloomberg*, 22 August 2008.
32 'Fannie Mae, Freddie "House of Cards" Prompts Takeover', *Bloomberg*, 9 September 2008.
33 'Mortgage Bailout is Greeted with Relief, Fresh Questions', *Wall Street Journal*, 9 September 2008; 'Treasury Briefs About Treasury Plan', *Japan Times*, 13 September 2008.
34 'Chinese Premier Blames Recession on US Actions', *Wall Street Journal*, 29 January 2009.
35 'Fannie, Freddie to Step Up Mortgage Bond Purchases', *Bloomberg*, 13 October 2008.
36 United States Department of Treasury, Statement by Secretary H. M. Paulson Jnr on Treasury and Federal Housing Finance Agency Action to Protect Financial Markets and Taxpayers. http://www.treas.gov/press/releases/hp1129.htm
37 'Stock Markets Soar After Freddie, Fannie Bailouts', *Washington Post*, 8 September 2008.
38 'Mortgage Bailout is Greeted with Relief, Fresh Questions', *Wall Street Journal*, 9 September 2008.
39 Statement by Secretary Henry M. Paulson Jnr on Treasury and Federal Housing Finance Agency Action.
40 'Fannie and Freddie Bank Losses Grow', *Financial Times*, 23 September 2008.
41 'Zhou, Trichet Endorse Rescue of Fannie, Freddie', *Bloomberg*, 8 September 2008.
42 'Asian Investors Welcome Paulson's Move', *Financial Times*, 8 September 2008.
43 'Asian Investors Welcome Paulson's Move'.
44 'China, Stung by Fannie, May Reduce Dollar Holdings, CIC Says', *Bloomberg*, 11 September 2008.
45 'GSE Regulators Says US Government Backing is Strong', *Reuters UK*, 23 October 2008.
46 'Western Banks Face Snub by China Fund', *Financial Times*, 4 December 2008.
47 'China Urges US to Stabilise its Economy', *Financial Times*, 4 December 2008.
48 'Fannie Mae Rescue Hindered as Asians Seek Guarantee', *Bloomberg*, 20 February 2009.
49 'Bernanke Endorses Some US Backing of Home Loans, *Washington Post*, 1 November 2008.

50 'Fannie Mae to Seek Funds from the Treasury', *Washington Post*, 27 January 2009.

## Chapter 6

1 B. Setser and A. Pandey, 'China's $1.7 Trillion Bet: China's External Portfolio and Dollar Reserves', Council on Foreign Relations Working Paper, January 2009. http://www.cfr.org/content/publications/attachments/CGS_WorkingPaper_6_China.pdf, p. 1.
2 Setser and Pandey, 'China's $1.7 Trillion Bet', p. 18.
3 'Chinese Forex Watchdog Burnt by WaMU Collapse', *Reuters UK*, 30 December 2008.
4 'Asia's Economies: From Slump to Jump', *The Economist*, 1 August 2009.
5 Quoted in, 'As Trade Slows China Rethinks its Growth Strategy', *New York Times*, 31 December 2008.
6 M. Goldstein and N. R. Lardy, *The Future of China's Exchange Rate Policy: Policy Analyses in International Economics 87* (Peterson Institute for International Economics: Washington DC, 2009), p. 33.
7 Goldstein and Lardy, *The Future of China's Exchange Rate Policy*, pp. 35–37.
8 'China: The Spend is Nigh', *The Economist*, 1 August 2009.
9 For the argument that there is only no alternative for China but to create an economy based on more domestic demand and with it yuan appreciation see Goldstein and Lardy, *The Future of China's Exchange Rate Policy*.
10 Quoted in 'Chinese Premier Blames Recession on US Actions', *Wall Street Journal*, 29 January 2009.
11 Quoted in 'Chinese Premier Blames Recession on US Actions'.
12 Quoted in W. J. Stroupe, 'The Not-So-Safe Haven', *Asia Times*, 17 March 2009.
13 'Wen Calls for US Fiscal Guarantees', *Financial Times*, 30 March 2009.
14 X. Zhou 'Reform the International Monetary System', *The People's Bank of China*, March 2009. http://www.pbc.gov.cn/english//detail.asp?col =6500&ID=178
15 Zhou, 'Reform the International Monetary System'.
16 B. Setser, 'China's Call for a New International System', Follow the Money blog. http://blogs.cfr.org/setser/2009/03/24/chinas-call-for-a-new-international- financial-system/
17 Congressional Budget Office, 'A Preliminary Analysis of the President's Budget and an Update of CBO's Budget and Economic Outlook', March 2009, pp. 1 and 11.
18 R. Byrd, 'Maxed-out Government Credit: Raising the Debt Limits on the United States', November 2004. http://byrd.senate.gov/speeches/byrd_speeches_2004_november/byrd_speeches_2004_november_li/byrd_speeches_2004_november_li_0.html

19 H. Clinton, 'Remarks by US Senator Hillary Clinton', 19 February 2008. http://www.realclearpolitics.com/articles/2008/02/clintons_wisconsin_primary_nig.html
20 H. Thompson, 'Debt and Power: The United States' Debt in Historical Perspective', *International Relations*, 21 3 (2007) 305–323.
21 'China: The Spend is Nigh'.
22 'Obama Nudges Hu on Currency', *Financial Times*, 17 November 2009.
23 H. B. Schwartz and L. Seabrooke, *The Politics of Housing Booms and Bust* (Basingstoke: Palgrave Macmillan, 2009).
24 L. Jacobs and D. King, 'America's Political Class: The Unsustainable State in a Time of Unraveling', *Political Science and Politics*, 42 2 (2009) 2. More generally on the institutional fragmentation of the American state in historical context see S. Skowronek, *Building a New American State: The Expansion of National Administrative Capacities, 1877–1920* (Cambridge: Cambridge University Press, 1982).
25 Kevin Gotham, 'The Secondary Circuit of Capital Reconsidered: Globalisation and the US Real Estate Sector', *American Journal of Sociology*, 112 1 (2006) 231–275.
26 See, for example, P. Hirst and G. Thompson, *Globalisation in Question*, 2nd edn (Cambridge: Polity Press, 1999); L. Weiss, *The Myth of the Powerless State: Governing the Economy in a Global Era* (Cambridge: Polity Press, 1998); E. Helleiner, *States and the Re-emergence of Global Finance* (Ithaca, NY: Cornell University Press, 1994); L. Mosley, *Global Capital and National Governments* (Cambridge: Cambridge University Press, 2003); D. Rodrik, *One Economics, Many Recipes: Globalisation, Institutions and Economic Growth* (Princeton: Princeton University Press, 2007); C. Hay, 'Globalisation's Impact on States', in J. Ravenhill (ed.) *Global Political Economy*, 2nd edn (Oxford: Oxford University Press, 2008).
27 See, for example, G. Garrett, *Partisan Politics in the Global Economy* (Cambridge: Cambridge University Press, 1998).
28 N. Philipps, '"Globalising" the Study of International Political Economy', in N. Philipps (ed.) *Globalising International Political Economy* (Basingstoke: Palgrave Macmillan, 2005), p. 16.
29 For a discussion of a similar point from a somewhat different perspective see N. Phillips 'Whither IPE?', in N. Philipps (ed.) *Globalising International Political Economy*, pp. 246–269.
30 For an analytical historical account of the interaction of the interdependencies created by trade and security issues see Ronald Finlay and Kevin O'Rourke, *Power and Plenty: Trade, War and the World Economy in the Second Millennium* (Princeton: Princeton University Press, 2008).
31 B. Sester, 'The Collapse of Financial Globalisation', Follow the Money blog. Available at http://blogs.cfr.org/setser/2008/12/29/the-collapse-of-financial-globalization/#more-4285
32 'Globalisation Under Strain: Homeward Bound', *The Economist*, 5 February 2009.
33 Goldstein and Lardy, *The Future of China's Exchange Rate Policy*, p. 69.
34 'South Korea: Second Time Around', *The Economist*, 23 October 2008.

# Index